Ancient Hawaiians carved many ki'i (images) to place in their heiau (t
represented various gods, whose supernatural powers were thought
them sacred. You may see replicas of these images during your visit to
more about the gods these images represent, read the story on pages 49-50.

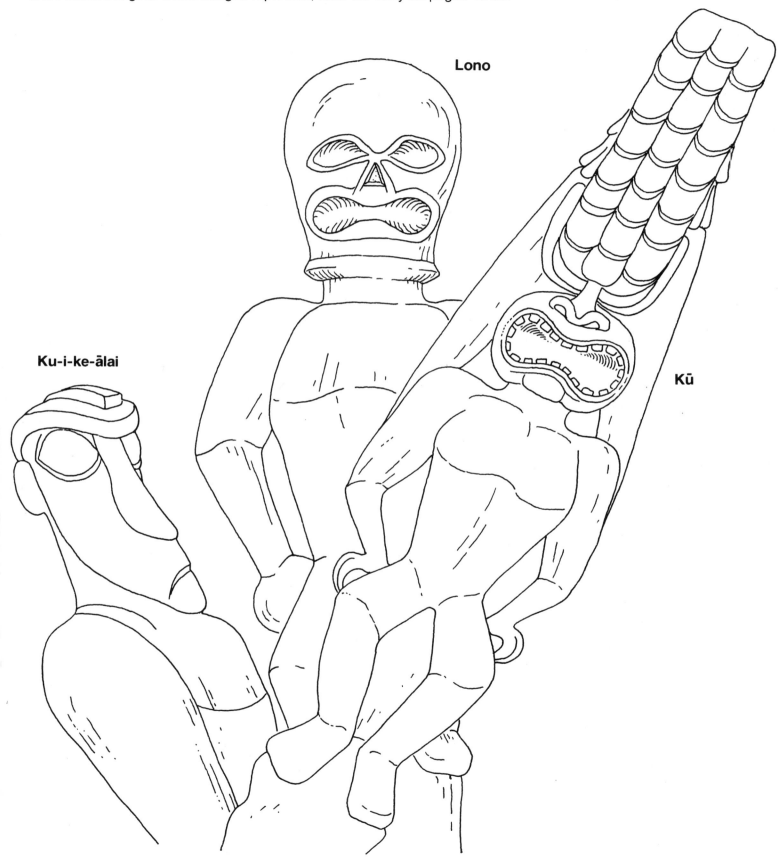

Lono

Ku-i-ke-ālai

Kū

THE Hawaiian Language

The language spoken by the people of ancient Hawai'i, and by many modern Hawaiians, is one of the most beautiful languages ever spoken. There are only twelve letters in the Hawaiian alphabet: A, E, H, I, K, L, M, N, O, P, U, and W. Almost half of these letters are vowels! This helps make Hawaiian sound pleasant, even poetical to listeners. Mark Twain described the sound of Hawaiian as "soft and liquid and flexible."

There are about 25,000 words in the Hawaiian language. By contrast, modern English has about 400,000, but you ordinarily use only a few hundred of these in your vocabulary. Modern English is remarkable for having a large number of words describing scientific and technological things. Hawaiian is just as remarkable for having a large number of words describing family relationships and certain aspects of the natural world. The vocabulary of each language reflects the lifestyles of the peoples they represent.

One of the attractive aspects of Hawaiian is that it becomes easy to pronounce with a little practice, once one learns a few basic rules. If you are unfamiliar with Hawaiian, the rules outlined below will help you to read Hawaiian words in the stories that follow.

HOW TO PRONOUNCE HAWAIIAN WORDS

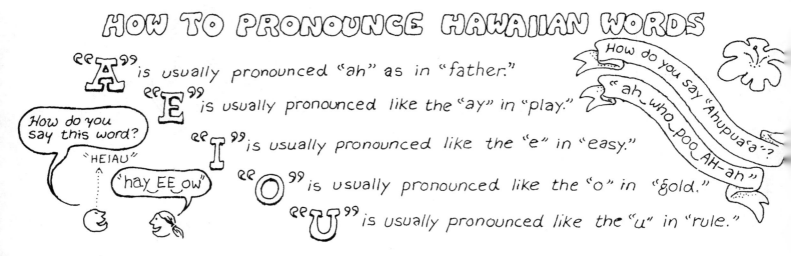

"A" is usually pronounced "ah" as in "father."

"E" is usually pronounced like the "ay" in "play."

"I" is usually pronounced like the "e" in "easy."

"O" is usually pronounced like the "o" in "gold."

"U" is usually pronounced like the "u" in "rule."

How do you say this word? "HEIAU" "hay_EE_ow"

How do you say "Ahupua'a"? "ah_who_poo_AH-ah"

macrons ~ Macrons are lines drawn over some vowels in Hawaiian words. They indicate a stressed letter. So the "o" in "Hōnaunau" must be pronounced slightly louder and longer than the other letters. If no macron is present, the stress is normally given to the second to the last syllable in a word.

glottal stops ~ Glottal stops are "upside-down apostrophes" separating letters, as in "Pu'uhonua." They indicate a place where one should pause in pronouncing a word. So the Hawaiian word for hill (pu'u) is pronounced "poo-oo" rather than just "poo."

Some ways of communicating today...

telephones

mail services

radio and TV

BOOKS

NEWSPAPERS AND MAGAZINES
Photos

INTERNET

computer modems

Some ways of communicating in ancient Hawai'i . . .

shell trumpets

pahu (drums)

pōhaku kikēkē ("bell stones"— make far-traveling noise when struck)

chants and hula

kūkini — (swift messengers)

HAWAIIAN ISLANDS

ĀKAU
(NORTH)

PUʻUHONUA O
HŌNAUNAU

The Story of
Hawai'i's Discovery

Volcanoes erupting from the ocean floor built up the Islands of Hawai'i over millions of years. Plants whose seeds could reach Hawai'i from distant lands quickly grew in the volcanic soil of the new islands. With the plants also came animals—mostly birds and insects. Relative to the age of the islands, human beings did not arrive until very recently. While the main islands began forming over 5,000,000 years ago, people have lived here only about 1,600 years!

Who were the first people to reach Hawai'i, and where did they come from? Long ago, before the start of modern civilization, tribes of people wandered across the world from one place to another. Sometimes they would settle, but often they were forced to move on because of unfavorable changes in climate, hostile invaders, or the hope of an easier life elsewhere.

Thousands of years ago, for unknown reasons, one such group of people migrated eastward from the region of Southeast Asia. They moved across Indonesia and the islands north of Australia. Their eastward migration was not continuous, but took place in short hops, following brief periods of settlement here and there. The pressure of other emigrants coming from the direction of Asia helped force them to continue moving. Finally, about 3,500 years ago, they sailed to the islands of the South Pacific Ocean. Here they settled and have stayed ever since. We call their descendants "Polynesians." The word Polynesia is a Latin word meaning "many islands," and it describes the ocean home of these people.

Like the Vikings of the Middle Ages, the Polynesians became skillful seafarers. They sailed in huge double-hulled canoes and navigated by observing the stars, the moon, sun, clouds, and ocean currents. Each canoe could carry dozens of persons, and enough water to last for weeks, or even months. From their first South Pacific settlements, the Polynesians traveled north, south, and east, occupying an area as big as North America, but made up, of course, mostly of water. Some of the islands were isolated by wide expanses of ocean. To reach Hawai'i, for example, Polynesians had to cross over 1500 kilometers (900 miles) of open sea. It seems miraculous that the Polynesians could have reached such places. Indeed, they were skillful sailors!

We don't know exactly why the first Polynesians came to Hawai'i. Perhaps fighting forced some of them to seek a new home, or maybe their population grew too big, so that some of them left to find new land. Perhaps it was just an accident. Because they had no written language, the details of the first voyage to Hawai'i are unknown. But historical tales, passed by word-of-mouth from one generation to another, tell us that there were two major migrations, one from the Marquesas Islands (3000 kilometers or 1800 miles away) about A.D. 400, the other from Tahiti (3500 kilometers or 2100 miles away) about A.D. 1200. These Polynesian settlers became the Hawaiian people, and part of their heritage is preserved today at Pu'uhonua o Hōnaunau National Historical Park. If you visit the Park you can learn much more about these interesting and gifted people!

The Hawaiians didn't have...

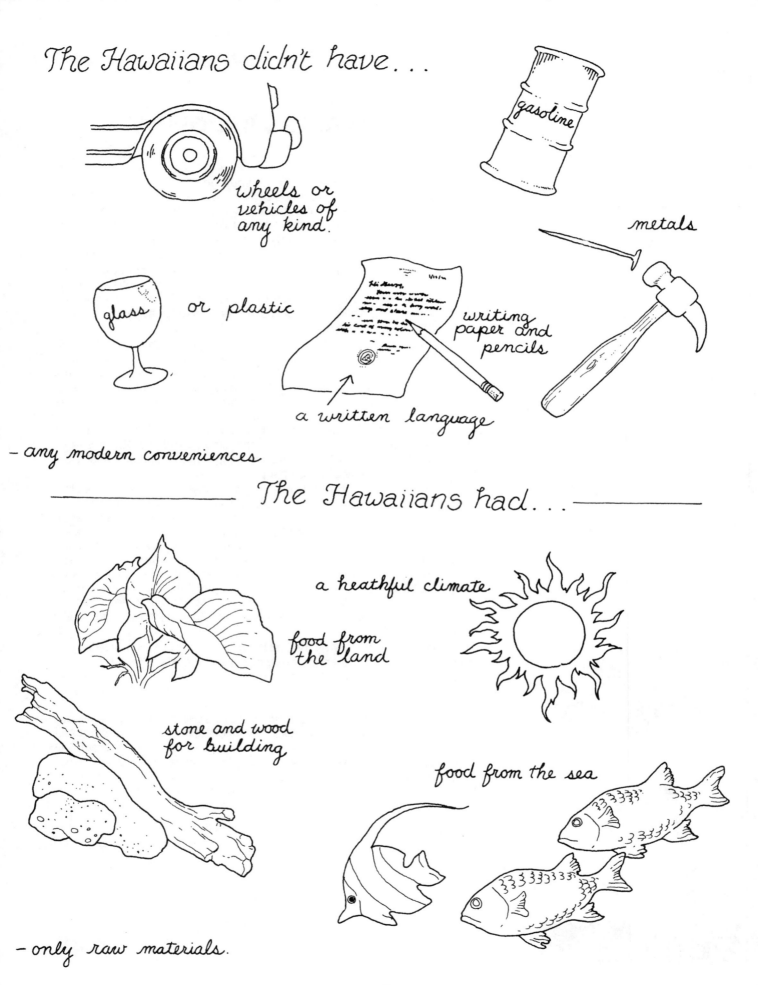

wheels or vehicles of any kind.

gasoline

metals

glass or plastic

writing paper and pencils

a written language

- any modern conveniences

The Hawaiians had...

a heathful climate

food from the land

stone and wood for building

food from the sea

- only raw materials.

The Hawaiians made...

The finest canoes in Polynesia

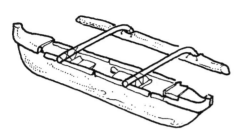

A wide variety of musical instruments found nowhere else

Many poetic chants and dances to honor their gods and chiefs and to celebrate love of life, nature, and people

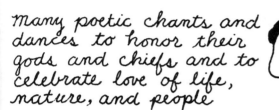

Feather work for ceremonial items, some of it the finest ever made

A wide variety of sports and games unique to Hawaii

The most advanced agricultural system in Polynesia, much of it based on irrigation

Superior quality wooden bowls and gourd containers

Excellent fishing implements and the only artificial fishponds in the Pacific region

For some centuries after their arrival in Hawai'i, the Polynesians continued to sail back and forth from the South Pacific to the Hawaiian Islands. The way of life in Hawai'i during this time was probably not greatly different from that throughout the rest of Polynesia because of the contact maintained by seafarers. But following the second great migration to Hawai'i around A.D. 1200, this contact mysteriously ended, and the Hawaiians become isolated from the rest of the world. During the centuries which followed, Hawaiians modified the traditional Polynesian ways of life and developed their own culture, in almost every way improving the things of the past. Some of the many accomplishments of the Hawaiians during this long period of isolation are shown on this page.

Island Life in Ancient Hawai'i

In order for the Hawaiian population to survive and grow, the limited resources of the islands had to be shared as wisely and fairly as possible. The major resources needed by the Hawaiians were soil, forest, and the ocean. To share these, the Hawaiians divided each island into sections of land. Each section, called an ahupua'a, typically began at the ocean and stretched inland to some prominent ridge or mountaintop. The coastline, farmland, and forests of each ahupua'a could be used only by the people living within the boundaries of the ahupua'a. In this way, a fair share of natural resources was available to each community of Hawaiians.

Although the land and sea were rich providers of food, farming, gathering, and fishing required long hours of hard work. Furthermore, natural disasters such as droughts or hurricanes could devastate a community by wiping out its source of food or its means of collecting it. Largely because of their strong dependence on natural forces, the Hawaiians governed themselves very strictly.

Each ahupua'a was overseen by an official called a konohiki who managed the land for his land holding chief. The konohiki decided who could fish in certain areas, supervised the building of agricultural projects such as irrigation ditches, drafted soldiers during wartime, took charge of community fishing excursions, and collected taxes. He was not elected by the people of the ahupua'a. Rather, he was appointed by the ali'i (chief). The konohiki was a trusted relative of the ali'i, and not always a native of the ahupua'a he managed.

Since there was no money in ancient Hawai'i, taxes and tribute were paid in the form of pigs, dogs, bird feathers (for ornamentation), bark cloth, and other items. After the konohiki collected a tax, he kept some of it for himself, then gave the rest to his chief, who in turn passed a part on to his superior, the district chief, called an ali'i-'ai-moku. The ali'i-'ai-moku in turn took some of the tax and passed the remainder on to the ali'i nui.

Except during time of war, the common people did not travel far from home. When travel was necessary it was usually done in a canoe. Sometimes persons simply walked. One or more footpaths encircled each island, connecting all of the ahupua'a together.

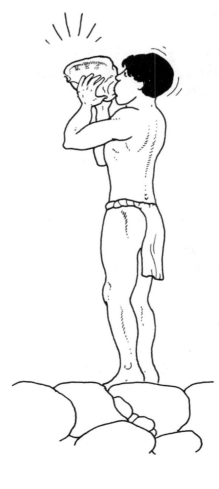

There were no cities or towns in ancient Hawai'i, only small villages mostly near the coast. Because people did not travel far, families tended to remain together for many generations. In fact, whole villages were typically made up of people related to one another in some manner. This family group was called the 'ohana. It was 'ohana that formed a foundation of Hawaiian society, just as single families form a foundation of our society today. Each 'ohana maintained its own fields and croplands, called a kuleana. This land was actually controlled by an ali'i and "loaned" to the 'ohana. As long as members of the 'ohana were productive and paid taxes, they could use the land.

There were no written laws or courts in ancient Hawai'i. Instead, laws were proclaimed by the ali'i and the kāhuna pule (priests). The ali'i made proclamations of non-religious nature called kānāwai. The priests proclaimed religious laws called kapu. The ali'i, like everyone else, were subject to punishment if they broke a kapu. Because of this, kāhuna were sometimes as powerful and influential as the chiefs themselves!

Here are some examples of kānāwai laws:
- a proclamation from an ali'i sparing the lives of all the warriors of a chief defeated in battle.
- a proclamation from an ali'i requiring farmers and fishermen to feed the hungry and to welcome strangers.

Here are some examples of crimes under kapu law:
- committing a murder.
- showing disrespect in the slightest for the person or property of an ali'i.
- making distracting noises during a religious ceremony.
- catching a certain type of fish at a certain time of year.
- as an adolescent or adult, eating with a member of the opposite sex.
- not praying to a certain god before starting an important project.

Kapu laws tended to be more far-reaching and numerous than kānāwai laws. Kapu designated and controlled the ways in which the gods should be worshipped and natural resources used. Like kānāwai, kapu also regulated many aspects of personal behavior and conduct. To violate these rules was to violate the sacred way of doing things, to "break kapu." This was often punishable by death.

Only a ceremony of purification by a kāhuna pule could remove the curse incurred by breaking a law. But first the lawbreaker had to reach a pu'uhonua, or "place of refuge," in order for the ceremony to be performed. The heiau (temple) and grounds of the pu'uhonua were considered very sacred, and once the lawbreaker reached the pu'uhonua he was protected by religious power, from the people who pursued him. But reaching a pu'uhonua was often not easy, as you will see!

How the land was used and shared in ancient Hawai'i—a typical ahupua'a

The volcano—builder of the island

Water from the sky

AHUPUA'A

Food and wood from the forest

Food from the soil

Path to other villages ←

Family group village

Path to other villages →

Canoe ramp

Food from the sea

Who's Who... in ancient Hawaii

THE **ALI'I NUI** (also called ALI'I 'AI AUPUNI) ruled supreme over the mokupuni (entire island)

EACH ISLAND was called a MOKUPUNI. Mokupuni were divided into MOKU (districts), made up of many AHUPUA'A. Ahupua'a were the land divisions on which typically several family groups ('OHANA) lived.

MOKUPUNI

MOKU

AHUPUA'A

THE KAHUNA NUI was usually related to the ali'i nui and was in charge of the priesthood. He was almost as powerful as the ali'i nui. He kept the religious image of the ali'i, and advised him on religious matters.

KAHU were also usually related to the ali'i nui. Kahu were attendents of the ali'i nui, serving as teachers and guardians of his children. Kahu lu kept the ali'i's regalia, and protected his possessions.

THE KALAIMOKU advised the ali'i nui on non-religious matters concerning his realm. He was responsible for making sure the ali'i 'ai moku and Konohiki (below) did their jobs, collected taxes for the ali'i nui, and supervised his major fishing and agricultural projects.

11

Each ahupua'a was managed by a KONOHIKI who was appointed by the ali'i nui and in many cases was a member of his family. The chief function of the konohiki was to make sure the people of the 'ohana kept productive in order to raise taxes for the realm.

KĀHUNA were trained experts in certain crafts or skills. They were found at all levels of society, from the kahuna nui and the priesthood to kahuna specialized at medical healing, canoe building, and tree cutting. The most dreaded kahuna were KĀHUNA 'ANĀ'ANĀ and KĀHUNA KUNI, who specialized in praying persons to death!

AHUPUA'A BOUNDARY MARKER— SOMETIMES A WOODEN IMAGE OF A PIG'S HEAD ON A STONE ALTAR

Each moku was ruled by an ALI'I 'AI MOKU, a district chief who shared the power of the ali'i nui by governing part of his territory. Beneath the ali'i 'ai moku were ali'i ai ahupua'a, lesser chiefs who each held an ahupua'a managed by a konohiki.

THE HAKU was an elder of the most important family of the 'ohana. He supervised the various activities of the families of the 'ohana, including their work, worship, and daily affairs.

KA PO'E—THE PEOPLE

THERE WERE TWO CLASSES:
(1) MAKA'ĀINANA were the common people of the ahupua'a. They lived by fishing and farming. Most Hawaiians were maka'āinana.

...and (2) KAUWĀ, the "outcasts" who were isolated on less fertile, unfavorable lands. Members of the small kauwā class were disliked and dreaded for unclear reasons, and were sometimes used as sacrifices in religious ceremonies and dedications.

'Ale'ale'a Heiau, Puʻuhonua, o Honaunau, Kona, Hawai'i

The HEIAU

Sacred places in ancient Hawai'i were often very simple. Fishermen, for example, typically worshipped single stones of unusual shape which were set in special locations for the worship of Kū'ula, a major god of fishing. At the other end of the scale were enormous religious temples, or heiau, such as those at Pu'uhonua o Hōnaunau.

There were several classes of heiau in ancient Hawai'i. Those to increase or "inspire" an abundance of fish or crops were most numerous.

Heiau hō'ola were temples where medical kahuna applied their practices to heal the sick and wounded. Each moku (district) usually had a heiau hō'ola.

Luakini heiau were the largest temples in Hawai'i. These were built by ali'i nui as places to house their images and to worship their gods. Here human sacrifices were performed, both to sanctify construction of the heiau, and as offerings to the god or gods honored there.

Finally there were pu'uhonua, or places of refuge. Here persons who broke a law could flee for protection and be freed of their curse by kāhuna who specialized in ceremonies of purification. Pu'uhonua were also places where persons not involved in fighting could take safe refuge during time of war.

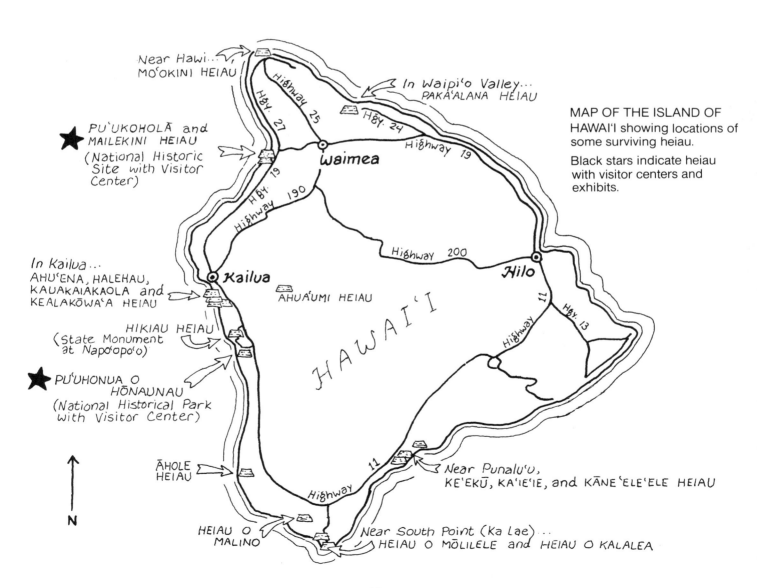

Near Hawi...
MO'OKINI HEIAU

In Waipi'o Valley...
PAKA'ALANA HEIAU

★ PU'UKOHOLĀ and MAILEKINI HEIAU (National Historic Site with Visitor Center)

MAP OF THE ISLAND OF HAWAI'I showing locations of some surviving heiau.

Black stars indicate heiau with visitor centers and exhibits.

Hwy. 27
Hwy. 25
Hwy. 24
Hwy. 19
Waimea
Highway 19
Hwy. 19
Hwy. 190
Highway 190
Highway 200
Hilo
Highway 11
Hwy. 13

In Kailua...
AHU'ENA, HALEHAU, KAUAKAIAKAOLA and KEALAKŌWA'A HEIAU

Kailua

AHUA'UMI HEIAU

HAWAI'I

HIKIAU HEIAU (State Monument at Napo'opo'o)

★ PU'UHONUA O HŌNAUNAU (National Historical Park with Visitor Center)

N

ĀHOLE HEIAU

Highway 11

Near Punalu'u, KE'EKŪ, KA'IE'IE, and KĀNE'ELE'ELE HEIAU

HEIAU O MALINO

Highway

Near South Point (Ka Lae)...
HEIAU O MŌLILELE and HEIAU O KALALEA

14

Pu'uhonua o Hōnaunau

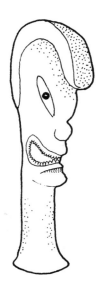

Pu'uhonua o Hōnaunau was one of the largest and most important places of refuge in the Hawaiian Islands. This reflected the fact that the moku (district) of Kona, in which Pu'uhonua o Hōnaunau is located, was the most heavily populated area in ancient Hawai'i. It is hard to imagine today that the somewhat barren landscape near the pu'uhonua was once dotted with dozens of villages inhabited by thousands of people!

The ali'i nui of Hawai'i and ali'i-'ai-moku of Kona lived for many generations near Pu'uhonua o Hōnaunau. One residential area inhabited by the family of a chief lay between the modern-day Visitor Center and the Great Wall of the pu'uhonua.

Pu'uhonua o Hōnaunau was not constructed all at once, but in several stages, beginning almost 500 years ago. Three heiau were constructed. The oldest lies close to the shoreline at the western end of the pu'uhonua and is now almost completely destroyed. 'Āle'ale'a, the second oldest heiau, lies near the center of the pu'uhonua. The stonework of this structure has been restored to its former appearance by the National Park Service. The youngest heiau is Hale o Keawe, at the northeastern corner of the pu'uhonua. Hale o Keawe has been rebuilt almost completely to appear as it did when the pu'uhonua was still in use.

The three heiau are enclosed by the Great Wall, built about 500 years ago as a boundary marker and also perhaps as a physical barrier to discourage pursuers from entering the place of refuge. All three heiau were not active at once, but at different times. The oldest heiau may have been abandoned when 'Āle'ale'a Heiau was built. Upon construction of Hale o Keawe, 'Āle'ale'a was also abandoned, possibly becoming a recreational area for chiefs and their relatives. Religious ceremonies were transferred to Hale o Keawe, which remained the only heiau active into historic times.

In many pu'uhonua, heiau were built to honor certain gods whose influence added protection to the pu'uhonua and made it sacred. The priests of the heiau took care of the pu'uhonua by maintaining the grounds and repairing damage from storms, high waves, and weathering.

A further form of sacred protection was provided by the chiefs themselves. "Hale o Keawe" in Hawaiian means House of Keawe, in honor of Keawe-i-kekahi-ali'i-o-ka-moku, an ali'i nui who ruled during the 16th century A.D. Bones of Keawe, and many of his ancestors and descendants were wrapped in bundles and stored within Hale o Keawe Heiau. Portions of 23 royal skeletons were deposited this way through time. The chiefs, kāhuna, and other important persons were presumed to possess special power, called mana, which gave them the ability to govern or perform their skills. Mana was a spiritual strength, a power also possessed by the gods. When a chief died, his mana did not die with him. Rather it continued to be associated with his remains. Thus the use of Hale o Keawe as a mausoleum for the chiefs gave the pu'uhonua grounds the additional protection of the mana of those chiefs, even hundreds of years after they ruled! For pursuers to chase their victims inside the pu'uhonua was to break kapu in a terrible way!

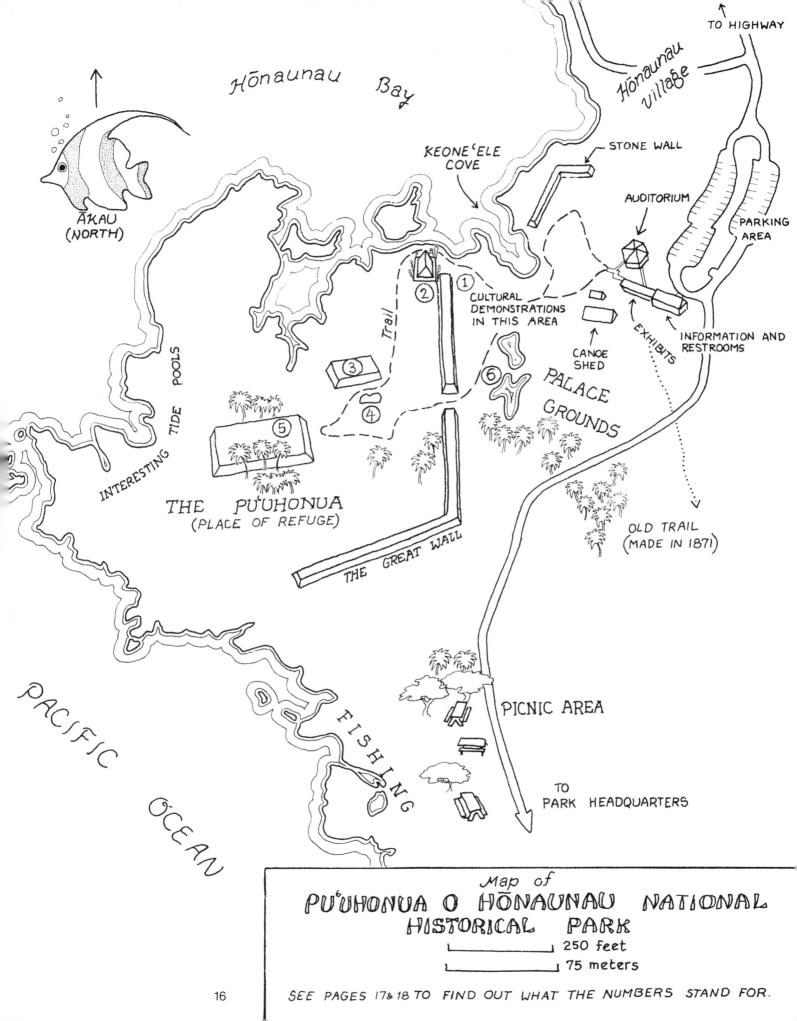

Hōnaunau Bay

KEONE'ELE COVE

STONE WALL

Hōnaunau Village

TO HIGHWAY

AUDITORIUM

PARKING AREA

ĀKAU (NORTH)

① CULTURAL DEMONSTRATIONS IN THIS AREA

②

Trail

③

④

⑤

⑥

EXHIBITS

INFORMATION AND RESTROOMS

CANOE SHED

PALACE GROUNDS

OLD TRAIL (MADE IN 1871)

INTERESTING TIDE POOLS

THE PU'UHONUA
(PLACE OF REFUGE)

THE GREAT WALL

PACIFIC OCEAN

FISHING

PICNIC AREA

TO PARK HEADQUARTERS

Map of
PU'UHONUA O HŌNAUNAU NATIONAL HISTORICAL PARK

250 feet
75 meters

SEE PAGES 17&18 TO FIND OUT WHAT THE NUMBERS STAND FOR.

① GREAT WALL

Built around 1550, this is one of the most massive walls in Hawai'i. It separated the pu'uhonua from the royal grounds. The skills of its builders are evidenced by the carefully fitted rocks. How do you suppose they moved such large stones without modern equipment?

② HALE O KEAWE HEIAU

This is the youngest of three heiau at Pu'uhonua o Hōnaunau. It has been partly restored by the National Park Service to appear as it did several centuries ago.

③ 'ĀLE'ALE'A HEIAU

Only the stone foundation of this heiau exists today. To learn more about this heiau, and Hale o Keawe, read the story on page 15.

A VISIT TO THE PARK

④

KA'AHUMANU STONE

According to a story relayed by Mark Twain, Ka'ahumanu, a wife of King Kamehameha I, fled to Pu'uhonua o Hōnaunau following a disagreement with her husband. She is supposed to have hid in an opening beneath this rock. The barking of her pet dog brought searchers to her hiding place! Soon she was reunited with her forgiving husband.

⑤

OLD HEIAU

This is the oldest heiau at Pu'uhonua o Hōnaunau. So old in fact that its name has been forgotten. A pile of rubble and some large stone alignments are all that remain of this ancient temple. Storm waves and tsunami have taken their toll.

⑥

HELEIPĀLALA (or LOKO I'A) FISHPOND

This is an example of a small fishpond such as was found at many sites in ancient Hawai'i. The Hawaiians stocked fishponds to provide themselves with a ready, easily maintained supply of fish. (Also read the story on page 8).

PICNICKING—A shaded picnic area is open to the public along the shore south of the pu'uhonua. (See map, page 16). This may be a pleasant place to relax after a tour of the park.

Things to do at Pu'uhonua o Hōnaunau…

FISHING—Fishing is permitted on a restricted basis along the shore south of the Pu'uhonua. Inquire at Park Headquarters for details.

SIGHTSEEING—Pu'uhonua o Hōnaunau presents some of the most picturesque scenery on the Kona Coast. If you own a camera, don't forget to bring it!

CULTURAL DEMONSTRATIONS—From time to time, Park interpreters give demonstrations of Hawaiian art and crafts, such as making fish nets, fashioning canoes, etc. Inquire at the Visitor Center for details and a schedule.

OTHER ACTIVITIES—Interpretive programs are regularly given by the Park Staff at the Park Auditorium. Inquire at the Visitor Center for details on all of the park's programs, publications, and hand-outs.

HAVE A NEW CAMERA? BE SURE TO PRACTICE USING IT BEFORE YOU MAKE A VISIT!

PHOTOGRAPH NUMBER 1

WHAT'S WRONG WITH THIS PICTURE?

Tips on how to have a good
visit at Pu'uhonua o Hōnaunau...

Coconuts can be large and heavy. Any falling coconut can be dangerous. Be aware of this.

SNAP!

OOPS!

!!??

Safety First...

The view is fine, but please don't try to climb the coconut palms!

WHUMP!!

Watch your step both on and off the trail. There are many rocks on the Park grounds. Near the shore be especially careful of slippery rock.

When exploring the shoreline keep a careful watch on the surf, or you may be swept away!

20

Pu'uhonua o Hōnaunau was once considered very sacred, and is still an important place for modern persons. Please have respect for the past.

Also have respect for the present, to help keep this place beautiful!

Follow these tips and enjoy your visit.

More About The Word "Pu'uhonua"

One translation of "pu'uhonua" is "sacred hill." The Hawaiians used "pu'uhonua" to refer to a place of refuge. This seems mysterious, because most pu'uhonua are not associated with hills at all. Pu'uhonua o Hōnaunau, for example, is located on a flat-lying coastal plain! Perhaps, though, this translation of "pu'uhonua" tells us something about how the word came to be used the way it did.

Throughout the South Pacific, early Polynesians built hill-top fortresses. In time of war, persons could seek protection here. It was difficult for a war party to capture a hilltop fortification because of rocks and logs rolled downslope by the defenders above. Perhaps the identification of hills with places of refuge became so strong Polynesians gradually began using the term "pu'uhonua" to describe any place of refuge.

In Hawai'i the term was used not only to describe hilltop refuges, but heiau such as the one at Hōnaunau, lava caves (called ana-pu'uhonua, or "cave refuges"), and even individual persons! A chief, for example, had the power to protect his subjects during time of trouble. He could also prevent one subject from being harmed by others, providing kapu were not broken, simply by commanding that the subject be forgiven and allowed to go free. For this reason, Kamehameha I, the ali'i nui who first ruled all the Hawaiian Islands, was sometimes called a pu'uhonua.

"Pu'uhonua" seems to be an example of a word which has changed in meaning with the passage of time. Can you think of some English words that have done this? (See page 71)

WORD SCRAMBLE
* * * * * * * * * *

SEE IF YOU CAN FIND THESE WORDS HIDDEN IN THE PUZZLE TO THE RIGHT! SOME WORDS ARE SPELLED STRAIGHT ACROSS (LEFT TO RIGHT). SOME ARE SPELLED VERTICALLY (TOP TO BOTTOM). OTHER WORDS ARE SPELLED DIAGONALLY, FROM UPPER-RIGHT TO LOWER-LEFT, <u>OR</u> UPPER-LEFT TO LOWER-RIGHT. GOOD LUCK! *(The answer key is on page 71).*

noni
wauke
hala
niu
pohokukui
kukui (<u>not</u> as part of pohokukui)
pahoehoe
ti
Lono
Cook
Kamehameha
kamaaina
Alealea
Heleipālala
kapa

WORD SCRAMBLE

```
O L U A L O A N K K A L K A U
M N O O K O N U P E N A K O A
N T O N O K K U U A M L N O O
H U W N O U A O W A W E N O P
K E P P I W U I A U I A P A A
A M L C I W U I P P L L A P E
M A P E O O N M A U O E H A I
E N U N I A O O W N P A O P O
H A A W O P U U T A P P E A U
A N N A K N A W W I U I H N O
M O N U L M H L N P A W O E W
E O W K A P A L A A O P E L E
H K I E P P L P P L O K E A W
A L O I A A A L A H A O P N M
M A U N A L O A O K E A L A N
L C P P A U A K I L O A M I M
L O N A I M U H A W A I I N N
O O N U I K A U A I O W N K O
K K O O U L E M E L E N N I M
I I W I I K A P O N O H A W U
```

22

Hawaiian CHANTS

❀ THE FOLLOWING VERSES HAVE BEEN TRANSLATED FROM ANCIENT CHANTS

A CHANT TO MOURN DEFEAT IN WAR

Fallen is the Aliʻi; overthrown is the Realm.
Gasping in death, scattered in flight
An overthrow throughout the land;
A hard panting from the rapid flight;
Countless the numbers from the universal rout.
The night declares the slaughter.
There extended lay my conquering night,
My own night, dark and blinded,
Falling on the path, falling on the sand;
The sovereignty and the land,
United in the Aliʻi, have passed away.
　—rephrased from a translation by Lorrin Andrews

A SURFER'S CHANT

Here comes the champion surf man,
While wave-ridden wave beats the island,
A fringe of mountain-high waves.
Spume lashes the Hikiau altar—
This is a surf to ride at noontime.

　—from a translation by Nathaniel Emerson

A CHANT TO EXPRESS THE JOY OF DANCING

Puna dances in the wind
As the pandanus groves dance in Keaʻau
Haʻena and Hopoe dance
The woman dances
Swaying near the sea of Nanahuki
Pure delight dancing
Near the sea of Nanahuki!

　—translation by Malcolm Naea Chun

A CHANT DESCRIBING RAIN

It was in Koʻolau I met with the rain;
It comes with lifting and tossing of dust,
Advancing in columns, dancing along.
The rain, it sighs in the forest;
The rain, it beats and whelms, like the surf;
It smites, it smites now the land.
Pasty the earth from the stamping rain;
Full run the streams, a rushing flood;
The mountain walls leap with rain.
See the water chafing its bounds like a dog,
A raging dog, gnawing its way to get out.
　—translation by Nathaniel Emerson

Who Set Up The Pu'uhonua?

Although the ali'i of ancient Hawai'i were supremely powerful rulers, they considered their own powers very small compared to those of the gods. For example, an ali'i could not control natural events such as the rains or volcanic eruptions. Nor did he have any say about kapu. What was kapu was defined by the kāhuna pule, and only kāhuna pule could plead with the gods to forgive persons who broke kapu.

But ali'i did have the power to create pu'uhonua. This was largely because of the way ancient Hawaiians viewed their ali'i as "protectors." To set up a pu'uhonua, all the ali'i had to do was declare a certain plot of land a sacred place of refuge. Heiau might later be built on this plot, but this was not always done. Some pu'uhonua were simply barren land! The pu'uhonua gave the ali'i and his people an opportunity to have the additional protection of the gods when the need arose.

Each moku typically contained a pu'uhonua. Thus there may have been several dozen pu'uhonua active at once in ancient Hawai'i. Both the ali'i nui and ali'i-'ai-moku could establish a pu'uhonua, but other persons, including kāhuna pule, could not.

If an ali'i were overthrown, the conqueror could not punish persons who sought refuge in the pu'uhonua of his defeated opponent; otherwise he would be breaking kapu!

Who set up Pu'uhonua o Hōnaunau? We will probably never know for certain, but most of the structures of the pu'uhonua were built early during the reign of the Keawe family. Frequently single families controlled an area for many generations. The Keawe family came to power early in the 16th century and dominated the island of Hawai'i until the arrival of European explorers. They made their "capital" the populous area at Hōnaunau, adding to the importance of the pu'uhonua there. Maybe Keawe-nui-a-'Umi, or his son Kanaloa Kua'ana, the first Keawe rulers, established Pu'uhonua o Hōnaunau; or perhaps they simply added structures to an area which had already been a place of refuge for many generations.

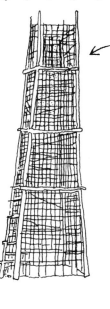

Lana nu'u mamao, or an oracle tower. Priests, and sometimes royalty, stood here during rituals. From the top floor of the tower, the high priest was supposed to communicate with the gods and learn of future events.

During rituals, the tower was sometimes dressed in a sacred cloth. An offering to the gods might be placed on the ground floor, as the priest stood above.

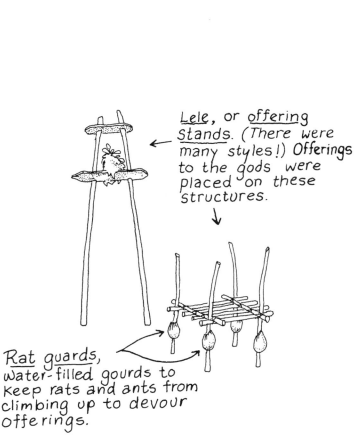

Lele, or offering stands. (There were many styles!) Offerings to the gods were placed on these structures.

Rat guards, water-filled gourds to keep rats and ants from climbing up to devour offerings.

SOME SPECIAL STRUCTURES of HEIAU

Secret Squares

A. CLOUDS AND SURF

B. KAMA'AINA (LOCAL RESIDENT)

C. PĀHOEHOE (ROPY) LAVA ROCK

D. KUKUI TREE LEAVES

THE PICTURES ON THE LEFT SHOW SOME OF THE SCENES YOU CAN SEE ON A VISIT TO THE PLACE OF REFUGE. THERE ARE OBJECTS HIDDEN IN EACH VIEW. CAN YOU FIND THEM? THE OBJECTS ARE DRAWN BELOW.

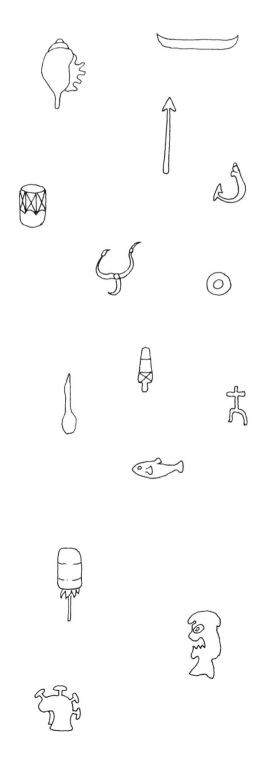

TSUNAMI!

The Hawaiians who lived on the coast feared a terrible natural threat—tsunami (pronounced sue-NAH-mee). The popular name for tsunami is "tidal wave," although this name is incorrect: tsunami have nothing at all to do with the tides. As the diagram below shows, tsunami are started by underwater earthquakes that cause major changes in the seafloor. The sudden changes disturb the overlying water which sweeps outward in all directions as a gigantic ripple. The ripple travels hundreds of kilometers per hour, and can cross thousands of kilometers of ocean. As it enters shallow water, it slows down and becomes a towering wave— sometimes as much as 15 meters (50 feet) tall in sheltered bays! Large tsunami batter Hawai'i once every few decades. The coast at Pu'uhonua o Hōnaunau is partially protected from their fury, but still has been struck by damaging waves in the recent past. The early Hawaiians had little or no warning of tsunami. Today a tsunami-alert system is in operation to warn people in time to evacuate.

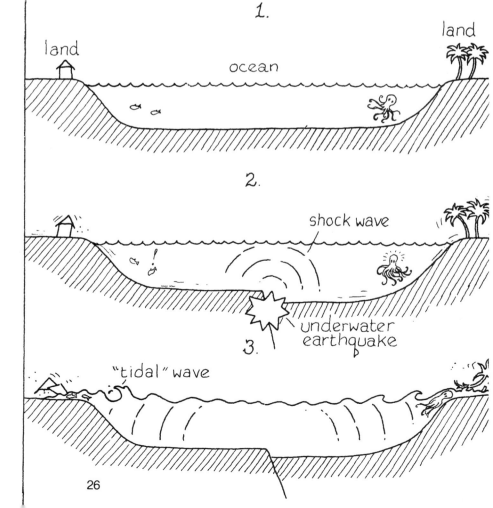

Journey around the Island

In ancient Hawai'i, all travel was done by canoe or on foot. To drive around the island today takes less than a day. Then, it sometimes took weeks to make the trip. Problems that might be encountered during travel are illustrated in this game. To play it, you will need one dice and a marker (like a pebble) for each player. Roll the dice to see who goes first. Each player takes a turn by rolling the dice and moving his marker the number of spaces shown by the number on the dice. If you land on a "Back 2" square, you must move your marker back 2 spaces to complete the turn. ("Forward" squares are obviously better). The first one to "Journey around the Island" wins!

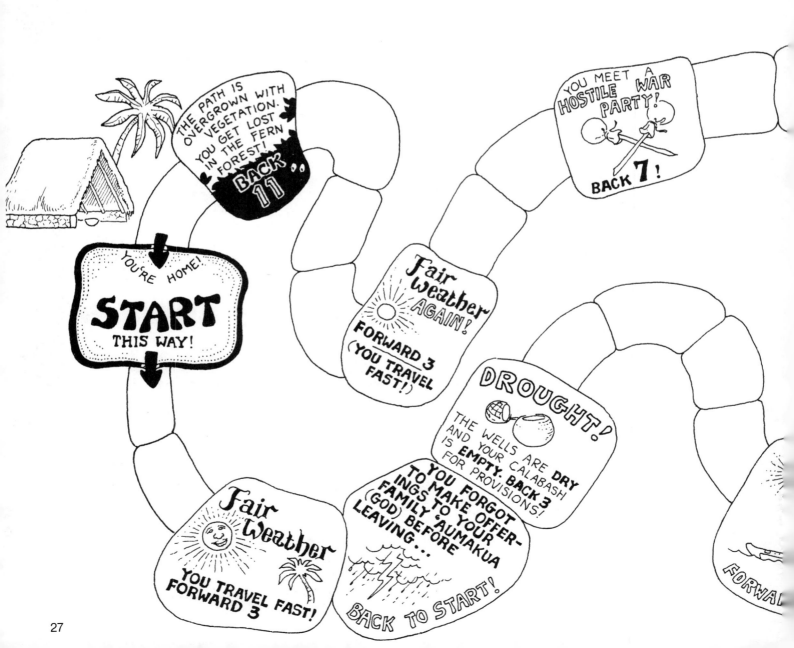

THIS MAP SHOWS ANCIENT DISTRICTS (MOKU) OF THE ISLAND OF HAWAI'I. TODAY, THE COUNTY OF HAWAI'I IS DIVIDED INTO THESE SAME DISTRICTS.

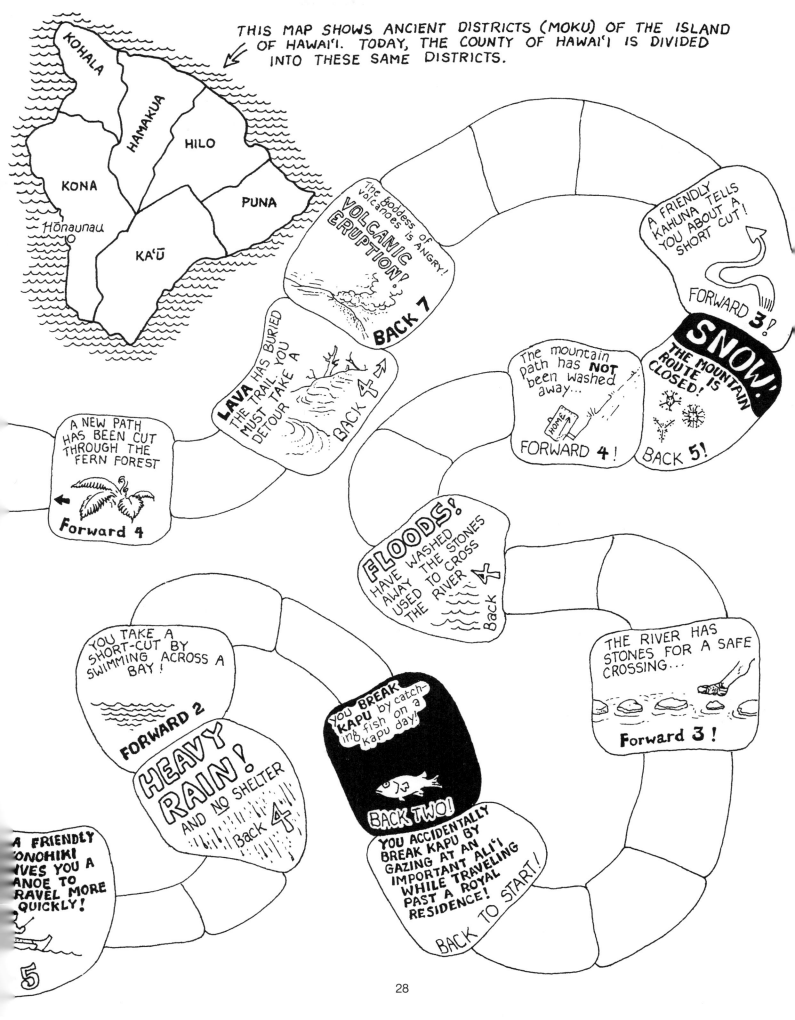

The Place of Refuge at HŌNAUNAU

A CARTOON STORY
BASED ON HISTORY!

THIS STORY BEGINS IN THE REALM OF KEAHI, AN ALI'I WHO CONTROLS PART OF THE ISLAND OF MAUI. IT IS SOMETIME HUNDREDS OF YEARS AGO. KEAHI HAS JUST FINISHED AN IMPORTANT MEETING WITH HIS MINISTERS AT THE ROYAL RESIDENCE! AS THEY LEAVE, THE OFFICIALS TALK WITH ONE ANOTHER —

OUR ALI'I HAS DECIDED TO GO TO WAR AGAINST KEALI'I, THE RULER OF KONA!

WARRIORS FROM HAWAI'I HAVE INVADED OUR MAUI HOMELAND FOR MANY GENERATIONS. NOW THAT WE ARE STRONG...

...WE MUST REMOVE THE THREAT OF FUTURE INVASIONS! WE MUST OVERTHROW KEALI'I AND CONQUER KONA! BY OUR CONTROLLING A PART OF THE ISLAND OF HAWAI'I, THERE IS LESS CHANCE MAUI WILL BE INVADED AGAIN!

WHY DON'T WE INVADE KOHALA? IT IS CLOSER TO MAUI THAN KONA!

THE ALI'I OF KOHALA IS MY UNCLE. I KNOW HE WILL BECOME OUR ALLY IF WE DEFEAT KEALI'I!

KANE-O-APUA, OUR NEW KAHUNA NUI, WILL SOON STUDY THE SIGNS OF THE WAR GOD. THEN WE SHALL KNOW WHETHER IT IS WISE TO FIGHT OR NOT.

KANE-O-APUA BELIEVES THE WAR GOD FAVORS KEAHI'S PLAN OF CONQUEST... THE ROYAL BODYGUARD PREPARES FOR THE COMING BATTLE!

BUT KEAHI CANNOT ACT RIGHT AWAY. IT IS THE MONTH OF 'IKUWA--THE KAPU DAYS OF THE GOD KŪ, WHEN FIGHTING IS FORBIDDEN EVERYWHERE SO PEOPLE CAN BEGIN CELEBRATING KA MAKAHIKI, THE ANNUAL HARVEST FESTIVAL. KA MAKAHIKI LASTS ABOUT FOUR MONTHS. DURING THIS TIME KEAHI'S MINISTERS GATHER TAXES. THEN KEAHI BLESSES HIS PEOPLE, GIVING THEM HOPE FOR ANOTHER FRUITFUL YEAR. FEASTING, GAMES AND HAPPY GATHERINGS TAKE PLACE FOR WEEKS!

WHEN KA MAKAHIKI IS OVER, KEAHI SENDS 'ELELE (MESSENGERS) TO THE KONOHIKI TELLING THEM TO RECRUIT WARRIORS FROM THE MAKA'ĀINANA AND SEND THEM TO AN ARMY CAMP NEAR HIS ROYAL RESIDENCE...

10 A FLEET OF WAR CANOES, MANY OF WHICH HAVE TAKEN YEARS TO CONSTRUCT, IS GATHERED AND MADE READY TO CONVEY THE ARMY TO THE COAST OF KONA...

11 KEAHI ALSO SENDS A MESSENGER TO HIS ENEMY, KEALI'I, ASKING HIM TO SELECT A LOCATION FOR THE COMING BATTLE! THE TWO RULERS DECIDE THEIR ARMIES WILL MEET IN NORTH KONA, ON A PLAIN NEAR THE FOOT OF THE VOLCANO HUALALAI.

12 IN THE MEANTIME, RITUAL SACRIFICES TO KŪ, THE GOD OF WAR, ARE PERFORMED. THE SACRIFICES ARE OFFERED UP IN A LUAKINI HEIAU.

13 NEARBY, IN A SMALL VILLAGE, TWO COUSINS NAMED KEAWE AND KALANI PREPARE TO JOIN KEAHI'S ARMY...

HMM...

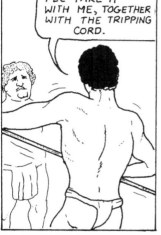

14 THIS SPEAR IS OLD, KEAWE, BUT IT IS STILL GOOD. I'LL TAKE IT WITH ME, TOGETHER WITH THE TRIPPING CORD.

15 GOOD, KALANI. NOW LET'S GET OUR FOOD AND WATER TOGETHER FOR THE MARCH TOMORROW MORNING. THEN LET'S PRAY TO OUR 'AUMAKUA, THAT WE MAY SURVIVE TO SEE OUR FAMILIES AGAIN!

16 NEXT DAY, THE TWO COUSINS DEPART FOR THE ARMY CAMP TOGETHER WITH OTHER MEN OF THE VILLAGE.

GOOD-BYE, PUALANI. TRY NOT TO WORRY... I PROMISE YOU I'LL BE CAREFUL!

BYE, MY BROTHER

17 GOOD-BYE, PUALANI... MY SONS WILL HELP YOU WITH THE IRRIGATION...

THANK-YOU, KEAWE.

18

19 INTO KEAHI'S CAMP COME THOUSANDS OF WARRIORS. MOST ARE MEN, BUT A FEW ARE WOMEN (WAHINE KAUA). LESSER CHIEFS (ALI'I AI MOKU), CHIEFESSES, PRIESTS, SERVANTS, AND NAVIGATORS ALSO ARRIVE AT THE CAMP. ◇◇◇◇

20 HERE KEAHI DISCUSSES BATTLE TACTICS WITH HIS FAVORITE WARRIORS...

21 ... AS GAMES AND CONTESTS ARE HELD TO TEST THE FIGHTING SKILLS OF THE ARMY.

21. EARLY THE NEXT MORNING, KEAHI ATTIRES HIMSELF ROYALLY AND ORDERS HIS ARMY TO BOARD THE WAR CANOES!

22. THE FLEET PUTS TO SEA CARRYING THOUSANDS OF PERSONS AND THEIR SUPPLIES SOUTHWARD ACROSS ALENUIHĀHĀ CHANNEL TOWARDS THE WEST COAST OF THE ISLAND OF HAWAI'I!

23.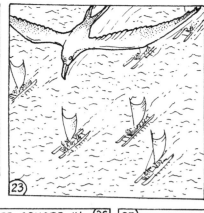

24. HOURS LATER, KEAHI CONSULTS HIS NAVIGATOR...

THE PEAK OF HUALALAI IS IN VIEW... LAND THE FLEET ON THE KOHALA SIDE, NEAR THAT WHITE SAND BEACH!

25. IN A CANOE NEARBY...

LOOK KALANI, THE ROYAL KAULUA IS PASSING CLOSE TO US! ...BUT BE CAREFUL YOU DON'T DISTRACT THE ALI'I BY STARING — IT IS KAPU!

26. THE ARMY COMES ASHORE IN NORTH KONA. THERE IS NO OPPOSITION. THE WARRIORS FIND THE LOCAL VILLAGES ARE ABANDONED. THE RESIDENTS HAVE FLED TO THEIR CAVE SHELTERS AND PU'UHONUA!

27. KEAHI'S WARRIORS LOOT THE ABANDONED HOMES FOR FOOD AND WEAPONS!

28. IT'S GOOD FOR US THAT THE PEOPLE LEFT SO SUDDENLY!

29. SHALL WE BURN THE VILLAGE?

NO! THE ALI'I HAS FORBIDDEN THIS!

30. NO VILLAGES MAY BE DESTROYED, AND NO RESIDENTS HARMED BEFORE THE BATTLE!

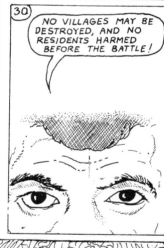

31. TO THE SOUTH, KEALI'I'S ALERT LOOKOUTS ENCOUNTER VILLAGERS FLEEING KEAHI'S ADVANCING ARMY, AND A SIGNAL IS SENT BY PUSHING A MASS OF FLAMING PĀPALA OVER A TALL PALI.

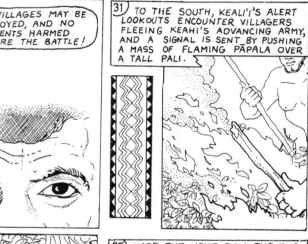

32. THE CASCADING EMBERS ARE SEEN SEVERAL MILES AWAY, IN THE FOREST CAMP WHERE KEALI'I HAS GATHERED A LARGE, WELL-PREPARED WAR PARTY!

33. KEALI'I'S WAR PARTY MARCHES NORTH TOWARDS THE PLAIN WHERE IT WILL FIGHT THE INVADERS FROM MAUI.

34.

35. LATE THE NEXT DAY THE TWO ARMIES MEET, FACE-TO-FACE, ON THE BARREN VOLCANIC PLAIN!

36. FOR SEVERAL DAYS THEY CAMP NEXT TO ONE ANOTHER AS OFFERINGS AND PRAYERS ARE MADE TO THE GODS OF EACH ALI'I. KEAHI'S ROYAL ASTROLOGER STUDIES NATURAL SIGNS TO DETERMINE THE BEST MOMENT TO ATTACK!

37. BUT KEAHI BELIEVES HIS ASTROLOGER HAS MISREAD THE SIGNS OF THE GODS, AND DOES NOT UNDERSTAND THE SITUATION.

38 KEAHI DECIDES TO ATTACK AT ONCE, BEFORE HIS ARMY RUNS SHORT OF FOOD AND WATER, AND BEFORE KEALI'I IS REINFORCED BY FRESH WAR PARTIES!

THE CLOUD PATTERNS HAVE BEEN ESPECIALLY OMINOUS!

39 I, YOUR ASTROLOGER WARN YOU, KEAHI, THAT IF YOU FIGHT TODAY, YOU WILL BE DEFEATED. MAUI WILL FALL HERE IN KONA!

40 "YOU ARE WRONG," REPLIES KEAHI. "THE IDOL OF KŪ SPOKE TO ME DIRECTLY IN MY DREAMS LAST NIGHT! HE SHOUTED A CRY OF ALARM--A BATTLE CRY! WE MUST FIGHT NOW!"

THUS DEFYING HIS ASTROLOGER, KEAHI SENDS A MESSAGE TO KEALI'I, "THE TIME HAS COME TO FIGHT!" KEALI'I AGREES, AND AFTER EACH CHIEF DISCUSSES HIS PLAN OF ATTACK WITH HIS WARRIORS, THE TWO ARMIES 41 ASSEMBLE MENACINGLY...

42 THE BATTLE STARTS WITH A VOLLEY OF STONES FOLLOWED BY IHE (SHORT SPEARS)...

SSSssSSHHH!

CLATTER

CLATTER

SSSSHHH

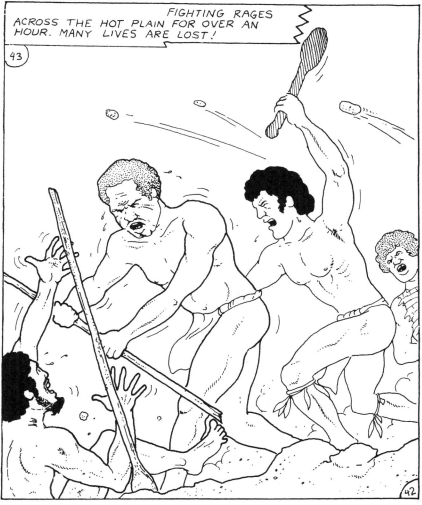

43 FIGHTING RAGES ACROSS THE HOT PLAIN FOR OVER AN HOUR. MANY LIVES ARE LOST!

42

SUDDENLY A GROUP OF KEALI'I'S WARRIORS SURGES TOWARDS TOWARDS KEAHI, WHO IS STANDING IN A DANGEROUSLY EXPOSED POSITION.

44

KŪ PROTECT US!

NO!!

45 KEAHI IS STRUCK BY AN IHE WHICH PIERCES HIS PROTECTIVE BATTLE MATTING! ENEMY WARRIORS RUSH IN TO SURROUND THE STRIKEN ALI'I!

LEI NIHO PALAOA, SACRED SYMBOL OF HIGH ROYALTY, IS SEIZED BY KEALI'I'S WARRIORS. 46

KEAHI IS KILLED! HIS

47

OUR SOLDIERS ARE FLEEING IN PANIC!

HORRIFIED, KEAHI'S WARRIORS BEGIN RUSHING FOR THEIR CANOES AT THE SHORE...

48

NO!

WE'RE ROUTED!

AAAAG

MOST OF KEAHI'S ARMY NEAR THE SHORE ESCAPES UNHARMED. BUT MANY OF THE WARRIORS FARTHER INLAND ARE SURROUNDED IN LITTLE GROUPS AND KILLED! SOME WARRIORS FLEE UPSLOPE TO FIND HIDING PLACES. KALANI AND KEAWE ARE AMONG THESE FORTUNATE SURVIVORS. FOR A WHILE THE TWO COUSINS HIDE IN A LAVA TUBE...

49

DID YOU SEE ANYBODY RUN INTO THAT CAVE?

SHHHH!

NO...LET'S MOVE ON.

50

WE MUST TRY TO ESCAPE TO A PU'UHONUA.

MY FATHER ONCE TOLD ME ABOUT ONE SOUTH OF HERE, ON THE SHORE. ...I DON'T KNOW HOW FAR AWAY IT IS, THOUGH.

51

THEY'LL KILL US IF WE'RE FOUND -- EVEN IF IT TAKES MONTHS TO FIND US!

LET'S STAY CALM -- TRY TO SAVE OUR-SELVES...

52

THE SUN IS SETTING... WE'LL BE SAFER AFTER DARK

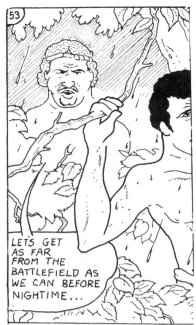

53 LETS GET AS FAR FROM THE BATTLEFIELD AS WE CAN BEFORE NIGHTIME...

KEALI'I'S WARRIORS WILL BE SEARCHING THAT AREA INTENSIVELY FOR SURVIVORS TOMMORROW MORNING!

54

55 NO FIRE, NO SHELTER.

WHEN DAWN ARRIVES WE MUST CONTINUE MOVING SOUTH, CATCHING GLIMPSES OF THE COAST AS MUCH AS POSSIBLE!

56 AT LAST THE RAIN'S STOPPED.

57 WE'LL HAVE TO TAKE TURNS STANDING GUARD THROUGH THE NIGHT. YOU SLEEP FIRST. I'LL WAKE YOU UP WHEN THE MOON RISES.

58 TOO COLD AND WET TO SLEEP!

GROAN

59 KALANI AND KEAWE PASS THROUGH A VERY UNPLEASANT NIGHT. THEY RESUME THEIR SEARCH FOR THE PU'UHONUA AT DAWN...

60 THERE'S NO FOOD TO BE FOUND HERE. WE'LL HAVE TO SEARCH FOR SOME AS WE TRAVEL...

OOW... SORE!

61 ANY THING SOUNDS GOOD TO ME RIGHT NOW. I'M STARVING TO DEATH!

NONI! THIS WILL KEEP US ALIVE EVEN THOUGH IT ISN'T VERY TASTY.

62 WHAT'S THE MATTER?

WHEW! SOME STINK!

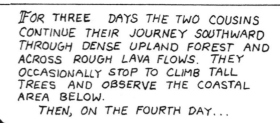

FOR THREE DAYS THE TWO COUSINS CONTINUE THEIR JOURNEY SOUTHWARD THROUGH DENSE UPLAND FOREST AND ACROSS ROUGH LAVA FLOWS. THEY OCCASIONALLY STOP TO CLIMB TALL TREES AND OBSERVE THE COASTAL AREA BELOW.

THEN, ON THE FOURTH DAY...

63 WATCH YOUR STEP!

64 LOOK! THAT MUST BE IT DOWN THERE--ON THAT SMALL POINT OF LAND! SEE THE WALL?... AND I THINK THOSE ARE WHITE FLAGS-- THAT'S A PU'UHONUA!

I THINK YOU'RE RIGHT!

67 NEXT DAY...

IT'S A WIDE LAVA FLOW... OUR FEET WILL BE CUT UP UNLESS WE HAVE PROTECTION.

LET'S MAKE SOME SANDALS!

65 THIS WILL BE THE TOUGHEST PART OF OUR JOURNEY, KALANI. THE LOWLAND IS CROWDED WITH HOSTILE PEOPLE... AND TO REACH THE COAST ANYPLACE NEAR THE PU'UHONUA, WE'LL HAVE TO CROSS THAT A'A LAVA FLOW BELOW--WHICH MEANS BEING OUT IN THE OPEN WHERE WE CAN EASILY BE SEEN!

66 KALANI AND KEAWE SPEND ANOTHER ANXIOUS NIGHT HIDING IN THE FOREST, BEFORE TACKLING THE PROBLEM OF CROSSING THE A'A FLOW.

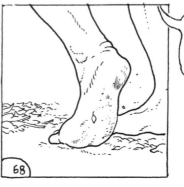

MAYBE THERE ARE SOME KI PLANTS NEARBY THAT WE CAN USE FOR MATERIAL.

68

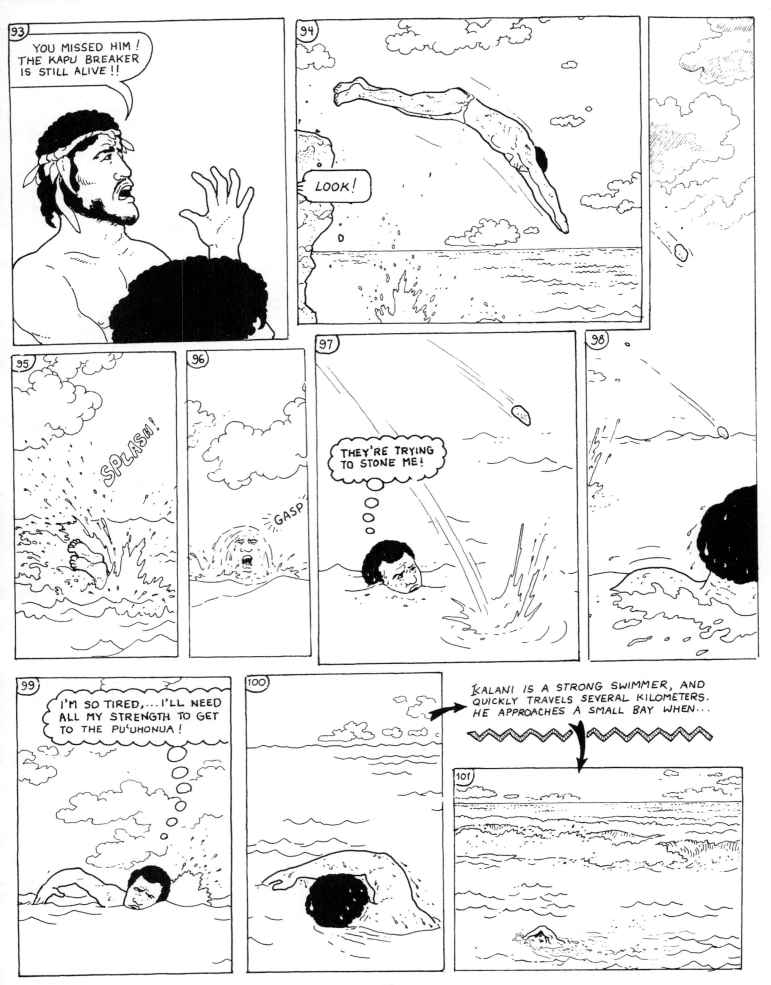

108 I'VE MADE IT! THE PLACE OF REFUGE!

109 I HOPE KEAWE ALSO MAKES IT... HE IS THE ONE THE ENEMY WARRIORS REALLY WANTED TO CATCH!

110

111 AFTER A BRIEF REST AND SOME FOOD, THE WARRIOR IS ESCORTED TO A KAHUNA PULE. HE TELLS THE KAHUNA THE STORY OF HIS ESCAPE.

YOU'VE BEEN FAVORED BY THE GODS YOUNG MAN. YOU ARE ONE OF THE FEW WARRIORS FROM YOUR MOKU TO HAVE SURVIVED THAT TERRIBLE BATTLE! YOU'RE SAFE NOW IN THIS PLACE OF REFUGE, AND IN A FEW DAYS YOU'LL BE FIT TO RETURN TO MAUI, FREE AND PURIFIED.

FOR SEVERAL DAYS KALANI REMAINS AT THE PU'UHONUA. AS HE REGAINS HIS STRENGTH, HE UNDERGOES A RITUAL, OR SEVERAL RITUALS, MOST KNOWLEDGE OF WHICH HAS BEEN LOST THROUGH TIME. THESE ARE PURIFICATION RITES LED BY KAHUNA PULE, WHO—THROUGH CHANTS—ATTEMPT TO COMMUNICATE DIRECTLY WITH THE GODS!

112 PERHAPS AT THE END OF THE FINAL RITUAL, THE KAHUNA PULE SAID SOMETHING LIKE THIS: "DESPITE YOUR COURAGE IN COMING TO THIS PLACE, YOU BROKE KAPU AND DESERVED TO DIE. YOU, KALANI, ENRAGED THE GODS BY SURVIVING THE DEFEAT OF YOUR ALI'I, KEAHI.

113 "OTHERS OF YOU BROKE KAPU DIFFERENTLY. FOR EXAMPLE, YOU, FISHERMAN, BROKE KAPU BY CATCHING AKU, A FISH YOU KNOW IS FORBIDDEN THIS TIME OF YEAR. AND YOU, FARMER, WERE CAUGHT EATING TOGETHER WITH YOUR WIFE!"

"NOW I'VE COMPLETED MY PRAYERS AND YOU HAVE A SECOND CHANCE... THE GODS ARE NO LONGER ANGRY WITH YOU. THE BURDEN OF BREAKING KAPU HAS BEEN LIFTED FROM EACH OF YOUR SHOULDERS! BUT MY EFFORTS WILL BE FUTILE UNLESS YOU HEED THIS COMMAND... YOU MUST LEAVE THIS PLACE THE WAY YOU ARRIVED, EITHER BY SWIMMING AWAY...

(114)

(115) OR BY DEPARTING IN A CANOE! YOU MUST LEAVE FROM THE SPOT YOU FIRST ARRIVED IN THE PU'UHONUA! AND FINALLY-- YOU MUST RESPECT, IN THE FUTURE, THE KAPU LAWS YOU BROKE. DON'T THREATEN THE WAY THINGS SHOULD BE. THE GODS ARE OFTEN UNFORGIVING. YOU MAY NOT BE BLESSED TO REACH SUCH A PLACE AS THIS AGAIN!

(116) CLEANSED BY THE KAHUNA PULE, KALANI LEAVES THE PU'UHONUA, SWIMMING NORTHWARDS TOWARDS A DISTANT SHORE. HIS FEELINGS OF RELIEF WERE MIXED WITH WORRY AND GRIEF FOR HIS COUSIN KEAWE.

BACK ON DRY LAND, HE BEGINS A LONG JOURNEY BY FOOT NORTHWARD TO KOHALA. HIS FORMER ENEMIES, KNOWING THAT HE HAS BEEN TO A PU'UHONUA, TREAT HIM WITH COURTESY AND RESPECT. FURTHERMORE, KEALI'I HAS ISSUED A KĀNĀWAI DECREE SPARING THE LIVES OF THE REMAINING SURVIVORS OF KEAHI'S ARMY! PEACE IS ALSO MADE WITH KEAHI'S NEPHEW, THE NEW RULER ON MAUI.

AFTER SEVERAL DAYS, KALANI REACHES THE NORTH SHORE OF KOHALA, NEAR UPOLU POINT. HE MEETS A FRIENDLY KONOHIKI CHIEF WHO OFFERS TO FIND A CANOEIST TO TAKE HIM ACROSS ALENUIHĀHĀ CHANNEL, BACK HOME!

(117)

REUNITED WITH HIS FAMILY AND 'OHANA, KALANI CELEBRATES HIS SAFE RETURN AT AN 'AHA'AINA (LARGE FEAST) GIVEN IN HIS HONOR

(118)

(119)

WHEN DID YOU LAST SEE KEAWE?

I LOST HIM WHEN WE FLED FROM ENEMY WARRIORS IN THE FOREST NEAR THE PLACE OF REFUGE. I CAN'T BE SURE HE'S ALIVE OR NOT...

42

BUT A FEW DAYS LATER...

120

BARK BARK

121

KEAWE!!! KEAWE IS BACK

EXCITEMENT FILLS THE VILLAGE AS THE NEWS TRAVELS. KEAWE HAS RETURNED ALIVE AND WELL! THE KONOHIKI ORDERS ANOTHER CELEBRATION OF HOMECOMING, FOR WHICH THE PEOPLE OF THE 'OHANA EAGERLY PREPARE!

TO KALANI, KEAWE RELATES THE TALE OF HIS ESCAPE...

122 "AFTER WE SEPARATED, THE WARRIORS CHASING US SPLIT UP, AS YOU KNOW! THE GROUP FOLLOWING ME CAME VERY CLOSE TO CATCHING ME..."

HURRY... I SAW HIM GO THIS WAY!

123 "I GOT DESPERATE. I HID INSIDE THE ROTTEN, BURNED – OUT TRUNK OF A KOA TREE. THE WARRIORS PASSED WITHOUT SEEING ME!"

124 "THE FOREST WAS SOON STILL AGAIN, BUT I KNEW THE WARRIORS HADN'T GONE FAR; THEY'D COME BACK ONCE THEY REALIZED THEY'D LOST ME."

125

I BACKTRACKED IN THE DIRECTION WE'D COME FROM.

126 "ON THE WAY DOWN THE MOUNTAINSIDE I SURPRISED A PARTY OF WOODCUTTERS! THEY SHOUTED AND THREATENED ME WITH THEIR ADZES AND CUTTING TOOLS! I DIDN'T STAY LONG..."

AUWE!

127 "MY PURSUERS WERE CLOSE BEHIND ME AGAIN. TO MAKE MATTERS WORSE, THERE NOW SEEMED TO BE FOUR OR MAYBE EVEN SIX OF THEM INSTEAD OF TWO!"

128. "NIGHT FELL. I SLOWLY FOLLOWED THE COASTAL TRACK TOWARD THE PU'UHONUA, BUT SOON SAW TORCH BEARERS BEHIND ME AND I THINK ALSO AHEAD OF ME IN THE FAR DISTANCE!"

129. "I JUMPED INTO THE FOREST AND, WELL OUT OF SIGHT OF THE TRACK, BURIED MYSELF IN LEAF LITTER AND BRANCHES."

130. "AS I FEARED, THE TORCH BEARERS WERE WARRIORS! THERE WAS A MESSENGER WITH THEM TOO, I'M SURE. HE MAY HAVE BEEN GOING TO ALERT OTHER AHUPUA'A ABOUT MY ESCAPE..."

131. "I DON'T KNOW HOW LONG I LAY ON THE FOREST FLOOR. I LOST CONSCIOUSNESS... MY SPIRIT WANDERED FROM MY BODY, PERHAPS FOR DAYS..!"

132. "THE NEXT EVENT I REMEMBER IS BEING AWAKENED BY A FRIENDLY STRANGER WHO TOOK ME TO HIS HOUSE, AND TOLD ME OF KEALI'I'S KĀNĀWAI DECREE SPARING OUR LIVES!"

133. "A MEDICAL KAHUNA TREATED ME AND BROUGHT ME BACK TO HEALTH. I THANKED MY HOST FOR HIS HOSPITALITY, AND AT LAST BEGAN MY JOURNEY HOME..."

"I NEVER REACHED THE PU'UHONUA. HAD IT NOT BEEN FOR KEALI'I'S DECREE, I WOULD HAVE BEEN KILLED! INSTEAD I WAS TREATED LIKE A CLOSE FRIEND--EVEN PROVIDED A GUIDE TO TAKE ME AS FAR NORTH AS KAWAIHAE."

134.

135. "IN KOHALA IT TOOK ME ONLY A FEW DAYS TO FIND A FISHERMAN TO TAKE ME TO MAUI. I MADE MANY OFFERINGS TO MY FAMILY GODS, TO KANALOA AND HŌKEO. BY THEIR PROTECTION I MADE IT HOME SAFELY."

KEAWE'S RETURN BROUGHT LIFE BACK TO NORMAL FOR HIS 'OHANA. THE NEPHEW OF KEAHI, WHO HAD BECOME THE NEW ALI'I NUI FOLLOWING KEAHI'S DEATH, WAS A WISE AND CAREFUL RULER. WARFARE DID NOT AFFLICT THE PEOPLE OF MAUI AGAIN FOR MANY YEARS. UNDER THE GUIDANCE OF THEIR NEW CHIEF, THE PEOPLE TURNED THEIR CREATIVE ENERGIES TO MAKING THE LAND MORE PROSPEROUS. KALANI, KEAWE, THEIR FAMILIES AND RELATIVES LIVED HAPPILY TOGETHER FOR A LONG, LONG TIME.

— The end

ESCAPE TO THE PLACE OF REFUGE!

YOU HAVE BROKEN KAPU! CAN YOU ESCAPE TO THE PLACE OF REFUGE?

start here!

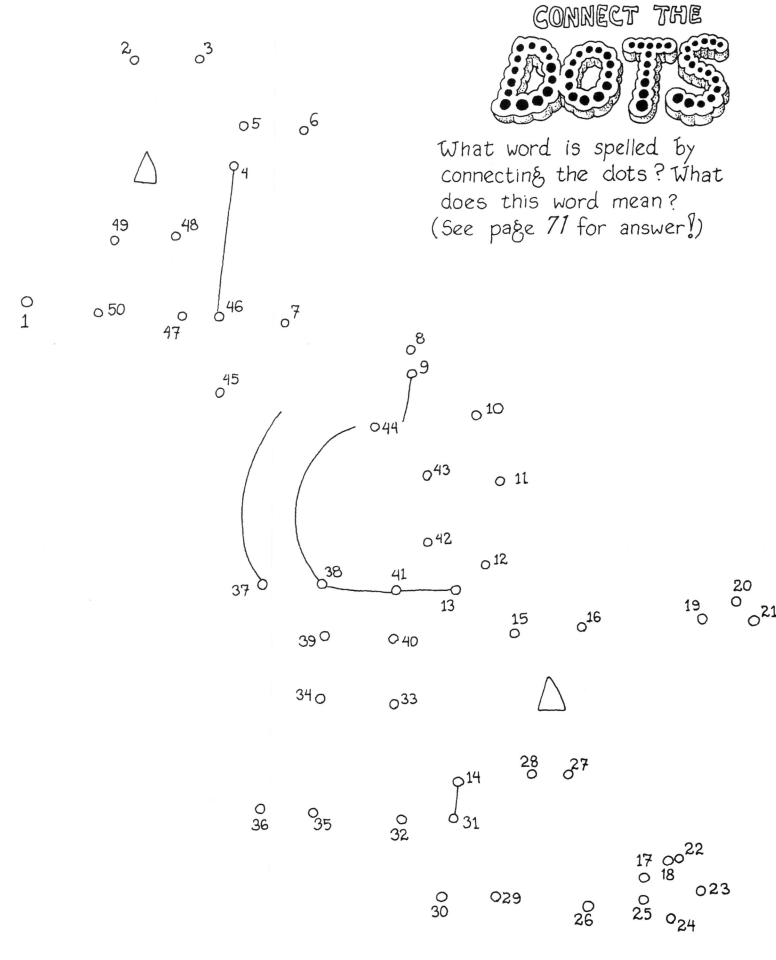

CONNECT THE DOTS

What word is spelled by connecting the dots? What does this word mean? (See page *71* for answer!)

PRESENT

GOLD ¢ $ ¢

BADGE

SYMBOLS OF IDENTITY

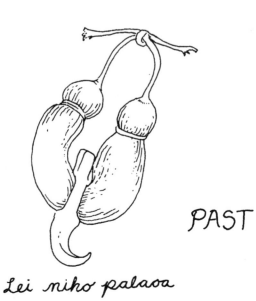

Kahili

Helmets

PAST

Lei niho palaoa

Kapu sticks

Symbols of Identity

There are numerous symbols of identity that surround us today. Examples include the American eagle, flags, badges and patches, the cross, the star, and many others. In ancient Hawai'i there were also numerous symbols of identity, but they were much different from modern ones. Some of them are drawn below and to the left.

According to David Malo, a famous 19th-century Hawaiian scholar, the objects of greatest value in ancient Hawai'i were the feather cape and helmet worn by the ali'i. Many helmets, called mahiole, were curved in a shape superficially resembling a rainbow—an important sacred symbol. Second in value was the lei niho palaoa, a royal necklace made from human hair and a whale-tooth pendant. The whale tooth was typically sculpted into a curving shape which may have symbolized the head of a god. The hook at the bottom perhaps represented the god's lower jaw. The third most important object was the kāhili, or staff with bird feather cap. This was carried by servants in front of the ali'i as he walked among his people. In this respect, a kāhili was similar to a flag carried at important ceremonies today. Each of these objects symbolized directly the mana granted to the royalty by the gods.

To symbolize kapu, Hawaiians set up crossed sticks topped with kapa cloth balls. These kapu sticks warned common people against entering forbidden areas accidentally.

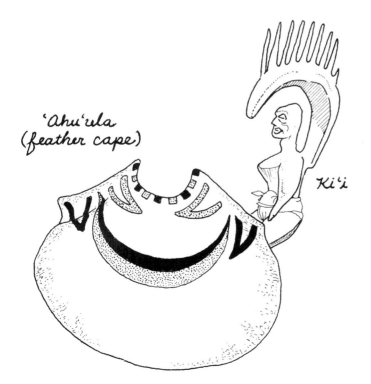

'Ahu'ula
(feather cape)

Ki'i

ARCHAEOLOGY HUNT

IN THE SCENE BELOW, THERE ARE HIDDEN PIECES OF EIGHT ARTIFACTS. CAN YOU FIND THESE PIECES? WHAT ARE THE ARTIFACTS THESE PIECES REPRESENT? (A PICTURE OF EACH ARTIFACT IS FOUND ELSEWHERE IN THIS BOOKLET! FOR ANSWERS, SEE PAGE 71).

Kua

Kūkaʻilimoku

THE GODS

Early Hawaiians believed that nature was controlled by powerful gods and goddesses. These deities often took living form as persons, plants, or animals with supernatural powers.

The Hawaiians worshipped four major gods. These were Kanaloa, Kāne, Kū, and Lono. Kanaloa was the lord of the ocean and tradewinds. He frequently appeared to people as an octopus or squid. Sometimes he appeared on land in the form of a banana tree. Early legends say that Kanaloa and Kāne traveled together through the islands making waterholes and fresh-water springs for people.

Kāne is the Hawaiian word for "male." Kāne was represented by the sun, rainfall, mountain streams, and all agents of health and healing. For this reason, Kāne was thought of as a "life giving god."

Kū was the god of the forest. Before launching a new canoe, the ancient Hawaiians prayed to Kū, because he gave them the wood and material for making canoes. Kū sometimes represented other things as well. Kūkaʻilimoku (Kū, "The Snatcher of Land") was the war god of Kamehameha I. Kūʻula ("Red" Kū) was the god of deep-sea fishing. Kū-i-ke-ālai (Kū "Who stands in the Way") protected many heiau. Kū was also worshipped by farmers who hoped to harvest good crops.

Lono was associated with thunder, heavy rain, and lightning. Hawaiians called Lono "The Thunderer," and referred to a dark cloud as being "the body of Lono." In animal form, Lono appeared as Kamapuaʻa, a pig. The Makahiki was an annual festival to celebrate the arrival of winter rains and give thanks to Lono. The festival lasted four months, and coincided with the time of paying taxes.

Besides the four major gods, there were less powerful but important deities like Pele, the goddess of volcanoes; Laka, the goddess of hula; and Kua, a shark god who had a red body. Thousands of other deities existed. Each played a role in the daily affairs of life. Hawaiian families also worshipped their own ancestors and ʻaumakua. ʻAumakua were personal spirits that guarded and protected each family. The spirits typically represented prominent ancestors.

Human beings were sometimes sacrificed to certain gods. These persons were usually criminals, prisoners of war, or other kapu breakers, though sometimes members of the outcast Kauwā class were sacrificed as well. But most offerings were in the form of food wrapped in kī leaves. Many Hawaiians still follow tradition and make kī leaf offerings to certain deities today.

Pele

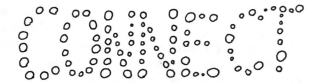 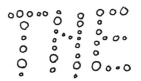 

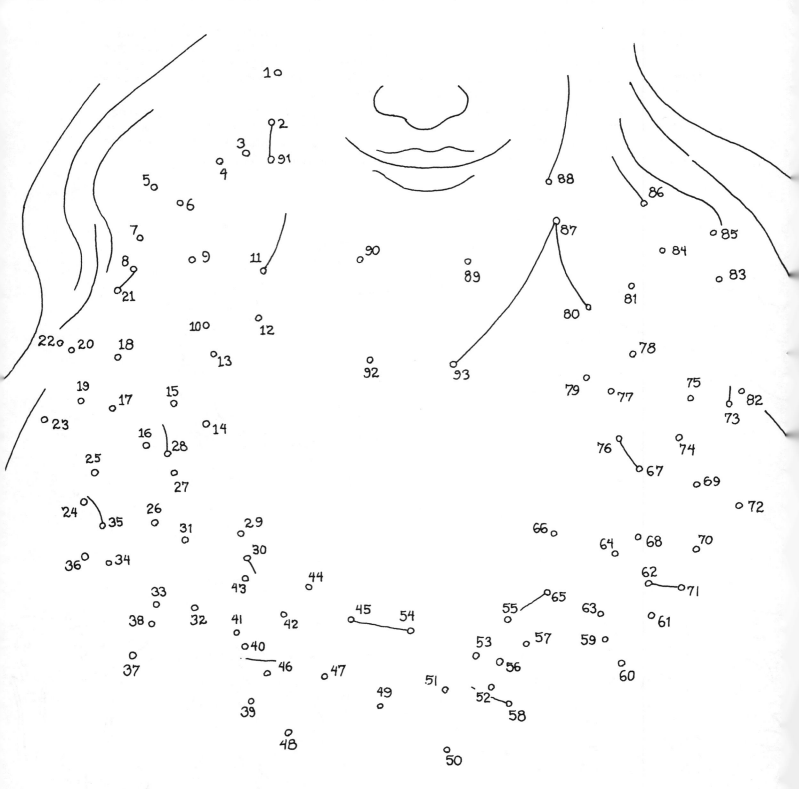

WHAT HAVE YOU MADE? _____

(Answer, page 71)

Kalai wa'a -- canoe making

Early Hawaiians made canoes from the wood of giant koa (acacia) trees cut in mountain forests and dragged by teams of men down to the shore. Stone adzes and chisels were used to carve out the hull. Then filing tools were used to smooth the hull. Finally the bottom was coated with paint made from a mixture of plant juices and charcoal.

Single-hulled canoes with outriggers were used by families for fishing. Double-hulled canoes up to 20 meters (70 feet) long were used for warfare and long-distance travel. Canoe making was very important in ancient Hawai'i.

WE CALL THIS TREE A CANDLENUT
TREE. THE HAWAIIANS CALL IT "KUKUI."

Some native plants, and how the Hawaiians used them...

nut of the kukui
(candlenut)

the pohokukui

a calabash

midrib of coconut
leaves used for stringing
candlenuts for lighting

The early Hawaiians learned how to use their limited island resources as much as possible. Probably the most valuable resource they had was plants. There were hundreds of types of plants known to the Hawaiians, and they put them to hundreds of uses. Shrubs and trees not only gave them wood to build with, but also gave them dyes, medicines, food, materials for clothes, fuel for light, and many other items.

As you follow the trail through Pu'uhonua o Hōnaunau, you will see several common plants that were of great importance in ancient Hawai'i. One is the kukui tree. Early Hawaiians sometimes used the kukui trunk to make wooden floats for fish nets, and, rarely, for constructing canoes. The sap was used as a glue, and sometimes chewed like gum! Dyes for kapa and

Niu, or coconut tree

basket woven out of coconut leaves

Kī, or Ti plant

54

stains for surfboards were also extracted. Oil from kukui nuts was burned in stone lamps called pohokukui to light up homes after dark. Sometimes the nuts were lightly roasted and the oily kernels were strung upon midribs of coconut leaves. These were lit to burn like candles.

Leaves of the kī ("ti") plant were used to make sandals, whistle-like musical instruments, hula skirts, wrapping to flavor meat and fish in cooking, and rain capes. They were also used as symbols of strong mana or kapu. Common people planted kī around their houses, because they believed it warded off evil spirits.

The niu, or coconut tree, was also important. The nuts were used for food and drink. The leaves were woven into baskets, brooms, and fans. Fibers in the wood could be used as strainers for food, or to make cords for tools and slings for throwing stones during battle. Coconut shells were made into drinking cups. Portions of the hollowed trunk were used to make drums.

From the ipu, or gourd, the Hawaiians made calabashes (containers) for storing food, water, and other items. The bark of the wauke was the favorite substance for making kapa cloth. Leaves of the hala tree were woven to make pillows, mats, and even canoe sails! Another plant, the noni, was a chief source of yellow and red dyes. Sometimes the people would eat the yellow noni fruits during famine to stay alive. The fruit juices were also used in a recipe for treating tuberculosis.

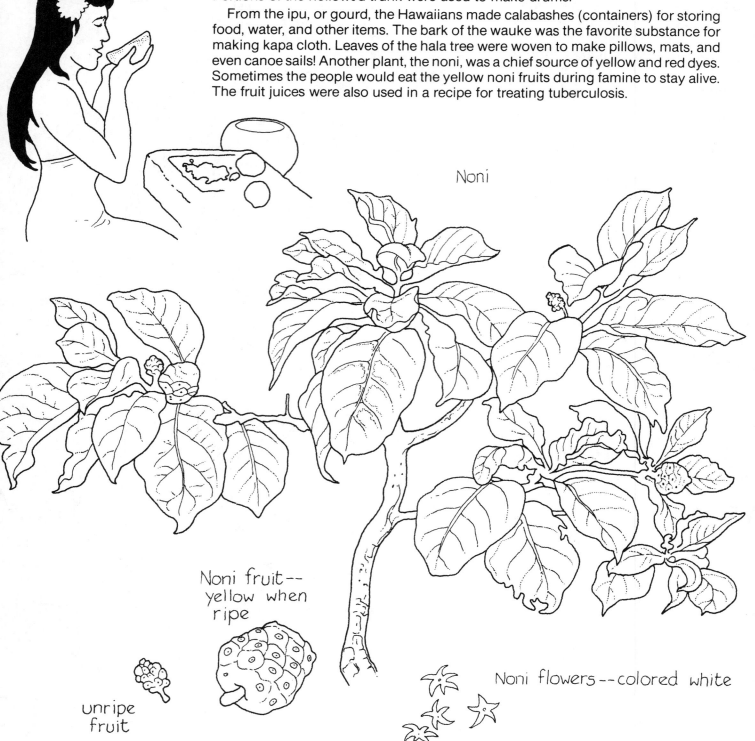

Noni

Noni fruit--
yellow when
ripe

unripe
fruit

Noni flowers--colored white

FROM THE LEAVES OF THE HALA TREE, EARLY HAWAIIANS WOVE FANS, PILLOWS, MATS, BASKETS AND OTHER OBJECTS.

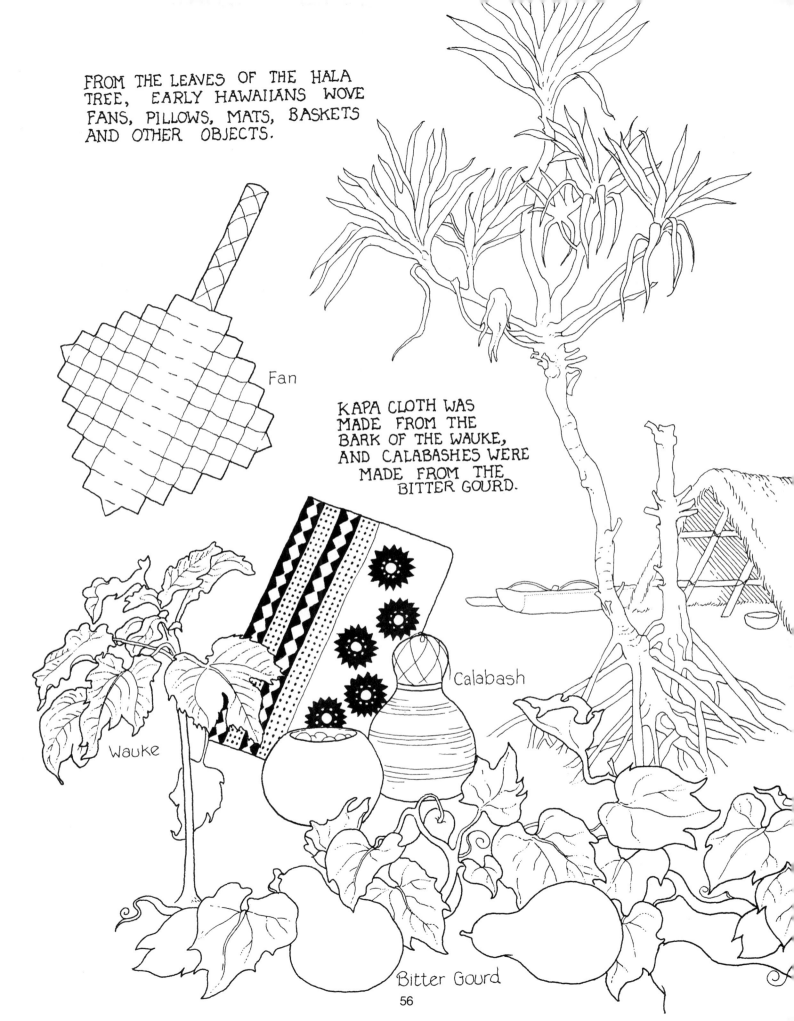

Fan

KAPA CLOTH WAS MADE FROM THE BARK OF THE WAUKE, AND CALABASHES WERE MADE FROM THE BITTER GOURD.

Wauke

Calabash

Bitter Gourd

(KA LAWAI'A)
THE FISHERMAN

Hawaiian fishermen used many techniques to catch fish. Woven basket-like fish traps may be seen as you walk along the shore or visit the fish ponds at Pu'uhonua o Hōnaunau. Fishermen also used spears. Sometimes spear fishing was done at night. The fish were attracted to the bright lights of torches carried by the fishermen, and swam in close enough to be speared.

Often an entire community fished together, using one giant net to catch the fish. This technique was called hukilau. Fish were frightened toward the shore as dozens, or even hundreds of people beat the water with lau (leaves, usually of the kī plant) and pulled the net in. Fish caught in the hukilau net were divided among those who helped. Some hukilau nets were up to 80 meters (250 feet) long!

Food Gatherers of Ancient Hawai'i

(KA MAHI'AI)
THE FARMER

The Polynesians brought many plants with them when they migrated to Hawai'i. These included the kalo (or taro), kō (sugar cane), 'uala (sweet potato), ipu'awa'awa (bitter gourd), niu (coconut palm), 'ulu (breadfruit), mai'a (banana), and other plants. Some of these plants were allowed to grow wild and were simply harvested when needed. Others, like the kalo, had to be cultivated. The only instrument used in farming was a digging stick called 'ō'ō. Most kuleana, where planting was done, lay just inland from the villages away from the shore. If you want to learn more about the kalo and other plants used by the Hawaiians, read the story on page 54-56.

LIVESTOCK

Early Polynesians brought pigs (pua'a), dogs (ī'lio), and chickens (moa) with them when they emigrated to Hawai'i. These animals served as a source of food for the settlers. They were allowed to roam freely around the villages and some were kept as pets. Some escaped to the wild. Goats, cattle, and horses did not exist in Hawai'i before the arrival of Western explorers and immigrants.

In addition to providing a source of food, animals served as sacrifices in religious rituals, and provided materials such as teeth, bone, and feathers for ornamentation and the manufacture of useful implements.

The Hawaiian Diet...

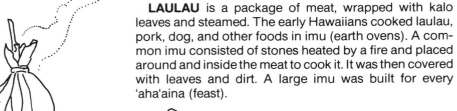

LAULAU is a package of meat, wrapped with kalo leaves and steamed. The early Hawaiians cooked laulau, pork, dog, and other foods in imu (earth ovens). A common imu consisted of stones heated by a fire and placed around and inside the meat to cook it. It was then covered with leaves and dirt. A large imu was built for every 'aha'aina (feast).

KALO (TARO) AND POI—Roots of the fully cooked kalo (or "taro") plant were pounded with water into a paste-like food called poi. It was served unseasoned, and most often, fermented. It was eaten simply by scooping it up with the fingers. Poi was the basic starch food and one of the main staples in ancient Hawai'i.

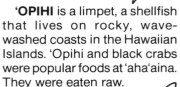

'OPIHI is a limpet, a shellfish that lives on rocky, wave-washed coasts in the Hawaiian Islands. 'Opihi and black crabs were popular foods at 'aha'aina. They were eaten raw.

I'A (FISH) were cooked or eaten raw. Some types of fish were reserved for royalty and kept in special fish ponds, as at Pu'uhonua o Hōnaunau. Others could be harvested only at certain times of year due to the kapu system. Octopus was also a delicacy.

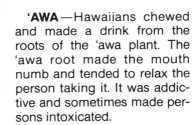

'AWA—Hawaiians chewed and made a drink from the roots of the 'awa plant. The 'awa root made the mouth numb and tended to relax the person taking it. It was addictive and sometimes made persons intoxicated.

WAI (WATER)—Fresh water was taken from springs, rivers, and rainpools. It was stored in calabashes (see page 56) for long journeys and periods of drought.

AND PA'AKAI (SALT)—To collect salt, Hawaiians evaporated seawater in shallow stone depressions. Some salt-lined basins can still be seen at ancient village sites near the coast.

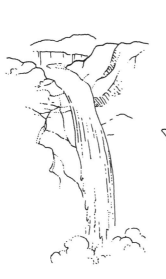

POHAKU KI'I (PETROGLYPHS) –

If you walk along the rocky coastline in Hawai'i, or follow old trails marked by smooth stones, you may discover some place where shapes have been carved in the rocks. These carved shapes are called "petroglyphs" ("pōhaku ki'i" in Hawaiian). The word petroglyph comes from two Greek words put together: "petros" for rock, and "glyphē" meaning carving. In some places only one or two petroglyphs may be found. In other places thousands occur together, concentrated in one small area!

Common petroglyphs include stick figures of people, canoes, artifacts, supernatural creatures, animals such as turtles, crabs, sharks, and dogs, and repeated images such as persons marching in a line. Many petroglyphs show shapes that cannot be understood without knowing about early Hawaiian customs. For example, circles with dots in the middle ⊙ were often carved in the rocks of sacred areas. The Hawaiians believed that if the piko (umbilical cord) of a newborn baby were placed within this type of petroglyph and covered with a stone, a long and righteous life would be assured for the child. This custom of hiding the piko of babies was followed by most Hawaiian families, although petroglyphs were not the only hiding places used.

A petroglyph in the shape of an open circle ○ might be carved by a traveler to indicate a journey made all the way around the island. If three travelers made this journey, a petroglyph like this ◎ might be carved. Sometimes the mode of transportation, such as a type of canoe, was also illustrated.

Many petroglyphs show action scenes, like people fighting or surfing. Petroglyphs showing the birth of children are also common. Straight lines carved in a rock might represent spears, sacred kapu sticks, or the umbilical cords of babies. Some petroglyphs simply do not have a meaning that we can understand.

Why did Hawaiians make petroglyphs? Some of them may have just been

a.

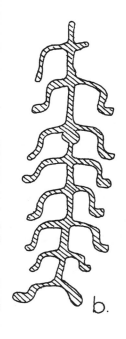

b.

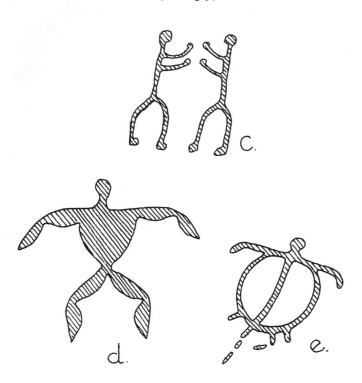

c.

d.

e.

doodles made by travelers and persons who felt a need to leave their mark. But carving petroglyphs required hard work with stone chisels, often under a hot sun. This effort, and the fine workmanship shown by most petroglyphs, suggest that Hawaiians had serious reasons for carving them. Perhaps they felt a need to record certain events such as battles, childbirths, or feasts in some manner other than by word-of-mouth. Could petroglyphs be a first attempt by the Hawaiians to develop written words and numbers? We'll never know for sure, but it's interesting to think about!

On these two pages are shown drawings of actual petroglyphs on the island of Hawai'i (labeled a, b, c, d, e, f, g). Can you guess what type of object each petroglyph represents? Turn to page 71 for the answers!

surfer wearing malo

What to wear in old Hawai'i!

Because the climate of Hawai'i is so warm and humid, the early Hawaiians usually wore very little clothing. Men wore a loin cloth, called a malo, and women wore a skirt, called a pā'ū. If the weather turned cold, as it does in the mountains during the winter, a clock-like garment called a kīhei was worn across the shoulder. The people usually walked barefoot, except when they had to travel over rough lava country. Then they wore sandals made of kī leaves and hau back.

Most clothing was made from the bark of the wauke, or paper mulberry tree. The important task of making cloth was given to women, who stripped bark from the trees and took it to houses set aside specifically for cloth making. First the strips of bark were beaten with wooden clubs until soft. Then they were mixed with water, allowed to season, and then again beaten by hand into the shape of a garment or piece of cloth. Finally the moist, thin layer was laid out to dry in the sun. The dried product was called kapa (or "tapa"). Many beautiful patterns were applied to the kapa to make it colorful and attractive when worn. The dyes were made from the juices of berries and plants.

During times of war or celebration, the ali'i wore colorful capes and helmets made from hundreds of thousands of bird feathers bound together. Individual capes sometimes took years to construct. It is said that the feathers woven into one cape worn by Kamehameha I were collected over a period of about 200 years! Red and yellow feathers were most desired and sought after by hunters. Only the highest royalty could wear feather capes. Captain James Cook wrote that their surfaces looked and felt like thick, rich velvet. Unfortunately many of the types of birds whose feathers were used in making capes and helmets are now extinct or rare. While modern diseases and destruction of habitat area has contributed greatly to destruction of native birdlife, some loss may have resulted from the hunting practices of early Hawaiians; by the time of Captain Cook's arrival, at least 26 species of native birds had already become extinct.

GROWING UP
in Old Hawai'I !

In the 'ohana every grown-up thought of each child as his or her own. Thus Hawaiian children had many "parents" and grew up in an atmosphere of much love and care. The mother and father of a child were often so busy working to feed, clothe, and support the 'ohana that their children had to be raised by grandparents or other close relatives. Because there were no public schools in ancient Hawai'i, grandparents taught children the skills they would need to know as adults. A girl (wahine) was expected to learn how to weave, make kapa cloth, work with plant dyes, prepare foods, cure sicknesses, and perform many other duties related to keeping house and raising a family. A boy (kāne) was taught how to fish, farm, hunt, prepare foods, make canoes, and fight as a warrior.

Until about the age of six, life was carefree for Hawaiian children. The children played many games such as kimo, uma, and holua kī (see pages 63-64). Boys and girls ate together with their mothers in the hale 'aina, a special house set aside as a place for women to eat.

making kapa cloth

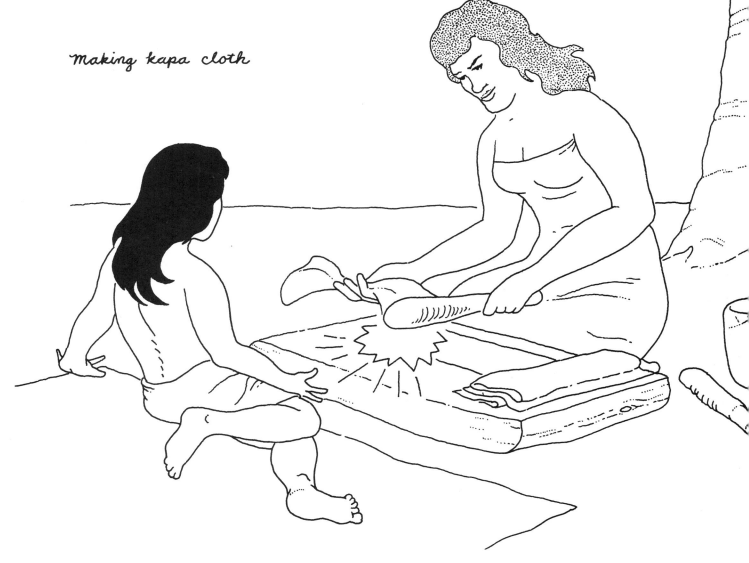

At about the age of six, boys were taken from the hale 'aina. After a special ceremony, a boy was proclaimed a man and allowed to wear the malo cloth (see page 61). Thereafter he always ate in the hale mua, a sacred house set aside as a place for men of the 'ohana to eat, and as a house for the family gods. His training for manhood had begun.

Eventually young people reached an age suitable for getting married. Little is known concerning the marriage customs of early Hawaiians. Mary K. Pukui, a Hawaiian scholar, wrote about marriage practices in her native moku of Ka'ū, after the arrival of Captain Cook: if a boy and girl wanted to get married they first made their wish known to their parents. Their parents then met privately to discuss such matters as where the newlyweds would live, what land and possessions they would use, and how they should support themselves. When these questions were settled the parents consulted their two children and asked if they approved of the arrangements made during the meeting. If a couple approved, the parents brought them together and married them. The parents commanded that the newlyweds take care of one another and also gave them practical advice about how to live together successfully. After this the bride and groom embraced and their wedding was completed.

In wealthy or royal families more elaborate weddings were often held. Preparation for these weddings included an exchange of rich gifts between the families of the bride and groom, construction of a wedding house and bridal litter, and gathering of food for a wedding feast.

According to Samuel Kamakau, another Hawaiian scholar, marriages typically consisted of only a single husband and wife. But in important families a man often had several wives, or a woman several husbands. In the ancient history of Hawaiians, such plural marriages are supposed to have begun when a man named Wakea, who was already married, broke kapu and took three additional wives. His wife Papa was so upset she married eight additional husbands!

Hōlua Kī--ti-leaf sledding

UMA is the Hawaiian version of "arm wrestling." On the command hoʻomākaukau! (Get ready!) players put their elbows to the ground and clasp hands. Elbows must be kept in position. On the command ʻoia! (Go!), each player tries to push his or her opponent's arm to the ground. The one who succeeds wins.

PĀ UMA is the Hawaiian form of "standing arm wrestling." The right foot of each player must be kept in position, with the two feet just touching. To win, push your hand to the chest of your opponent first. If your right foot moves, you lose automatically. Be careful not to lose your balance.

In another version of pā uma, you win by pulling your opponent's hand to your chest first. Use the same commands as in uma.

KIMO is a game similar to jacks, but is not played with jackstones and a rubber ball. Instead it is played with fifty or a hundred small, rounded pebbles called ʻai, and a stone for tossing, called a kimo. Toss the kimo into the air, quickly pick up a pebble from the ʻai pile, then catch the kimo with the same hand before it hits the ground. You have "won" the pebble if you catch the kimo before it hits. Then let your opponent take his turn. The player who has won the most pebbles when the pile is gone has won the game.

HAWAIIAN GAMES
YOU CAN PLAY!

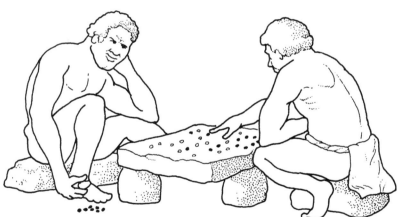

KŌNANE is a Hawaiian game similar to checkers. Kamehameha I was one of Hawaiʻi's best kōnane players. You may see several kōnane boards carved into the rocks at Puʻuhonua o Hōnaunau. The game was played with about 64 pieces—usually 32 black lava pebbles and 32 white coral pebbles. As in checkers, one wins by jumping an opponent's pieces. Ask a Ranger at the Visitor Center for instructions on how to play kōnane; then you can play a game during your visit to the Park!

HAWAIIAN CROSSWORD

All the words used in the crossword are Hawaiian. You will find them mentioned elsewhere in this book (Answer Key, page 71).

ACROSS

1. The largest island in the Hawaiian Islands
3. Hawaiian word for "hello," "farewell," and "love."
5. Name for leader in ancient Hawai'i.
7. This game is like checkers.
9. Plant roots make this food.
11. A drink is made from roots of this plant.
13. To make baskets, collect leaves of this tree.
15. Hill
17. A religious official
19. Shellfish
21. Land division
23. Ceremonial dance of ancient Hawai'i

DOWN

2. A king must have this to rule his people.
4. Same as 3-across
6. Land
7. A whistle was made from leaves of this plant.
8. Worn by men
10. A "foundation" of ancient Hawaiian society
12. Wooden idols were made from wood of this tree.
14. Watch out for falling_____! (Use Hawaiian word for the tree.)
16. "Church" in ancient Hawai'i
17. Hawaiians prayed to this god before launching new canoes.
18. The Place of Refuge at _____
20. ___ 'awa'awa
22. Set of religious laws
24. Breadfruit
25. This was in progress when Captain Cook arrived.

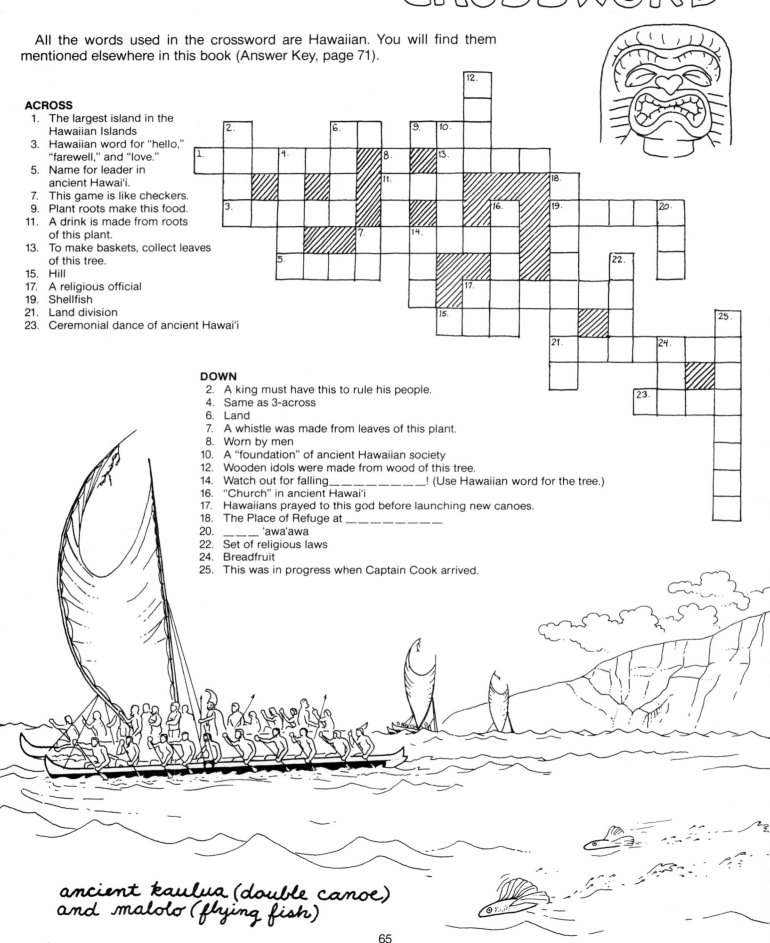

ancient kaulua (double canoe) and malolo (flying fish)

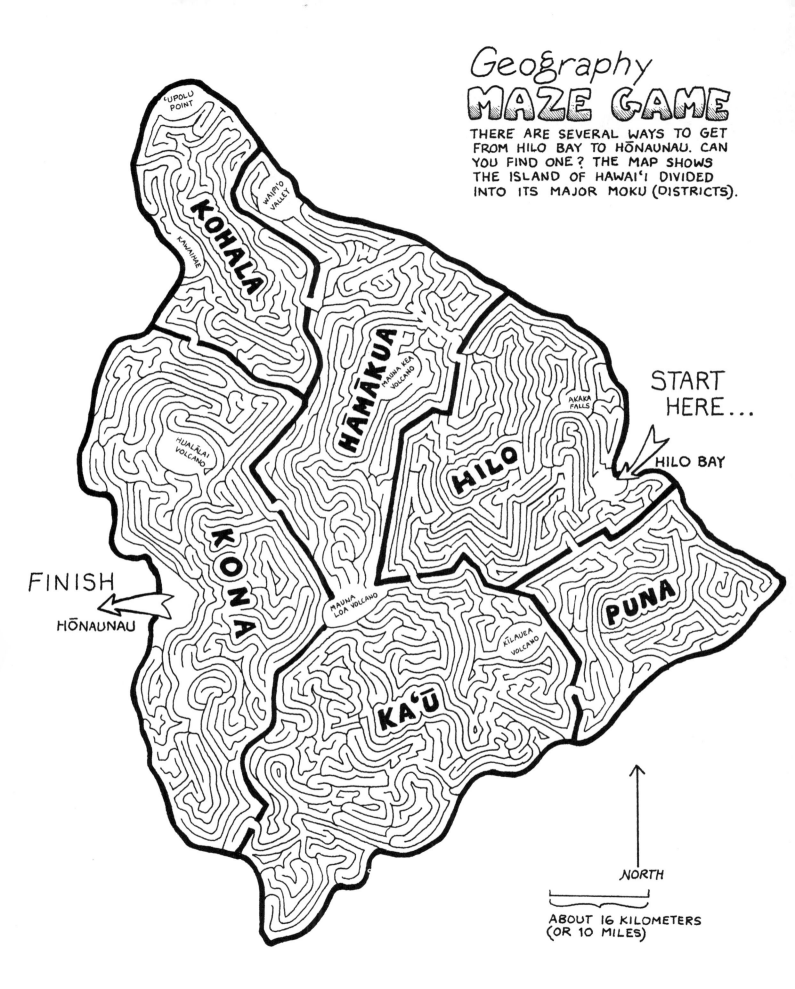

Geography
MAZE GAME

THERE ARE SEVERAL WAYS TO GET FROM HILO BAY TO HŌNAUNAU. CAN YOU FIND ONE? THE MAP SHOWS THE ISLAND OF HAWAI'I DIVIDED INTO ITS MAJOR MOKU (DISTRICTS).

'UPOLU POINT

KOHALA

KAWAIHAE

WAIPI'O VALLEY

HĀMĀKUA

MAUNA KEA VOLCANO

AKAKA FALLS

START HERE...

HILO

HILO BAY

HUALĀLAI VOLCANO

KONA

FINISH

HŌNAUNAU

MAUNA LOA VOLCANO

PUNA

KĪLAUEA VOLCANO

KA'Ū

NORTH

ABOUT 16 KILOMETERS (OR 10 MILES)

MYSTERIOUS TIDEPOOLS

There are many tidepools and inlets filled with interesting forms of life along the shore at Pu'uhonua o Hōnaunau. Try to find these as you explore: a) crab, b) coral (white to tan-colored), c) brain coral (shaped like a brain), d) worm tube (gray to white), e) tropical fish, f) limpet shell (shaped like a volcano), g) snail shell, h) hermit crab. You can make a game of exploring; whoever discovers all of these objects first, wins!

Around many of the tidepools there are huge rocks lying on the lava. How do you suppose they got here? (Answer, page 71)

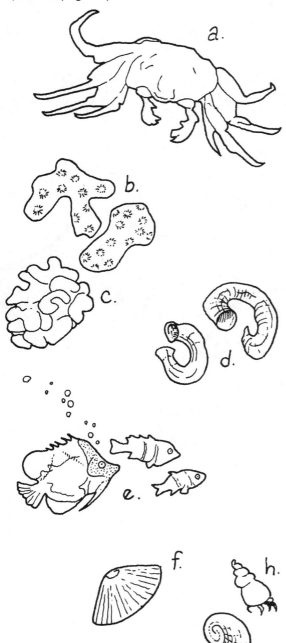

OBSERVE AND LEARN...!

As you visit Pu'uhonua o Hōnaunau you may see many new and different things that arouse your curiosity. During your visit, consider the questions below. Can you think of any answers for them? Try to make up answers, then look on page 71. (You may also ask a Park Ranger for help).

a) Why do you think the door to Hale o Keawe is so small?

b) Why do the wood carvings (ki'i) that surround Hale o Keawe look so mean rather than smiling and laughing?

TREE MOLD WITH RIDGED MARKINGS INSIDE. (TINY ARROW POINTS TO ONE MARKING).

c) What caused the ridge-like markings on the tree molds near the visitor Center?

d) Why are the largest rocks usually at the bottom and corners of the Great Wall and the smallest at the top?

e) Look at the thatching of the leaves forming the roof of the canoe shed. Why is the thatching like this...

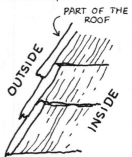

and not like this...

Can you think of other questions to ask? You may be surprised at how much you can learn from seeking the answers to them!

A.D. 1778

The Story of Modern Hawai'i

In the 18th century (A.D. 1701-1800), the countries of Europe were the most powerful in the world. In particular, England, France, and Russia were expanding their empires over much of the globe. This was a great century for European explorers, because there was still much new land for them to discover and prepare for colonization.

One of the foremost explorers was Captain James Cook of the Royal British Navy. He made very accurate charts and maps of coastlines, and collected much valuable information for future navigators. Three times the British Admiralty sent Captain Cook to explore the Pacific to find new lands and passageways. On his third voyage, in 1778, he discovered Hawai'i. Then, in January, 1779, his ships sailed into Kealakekua Bay, six and a half kilometers (four miles) north of Pu'uhonua o Hōnaunau. The British arrived while the Hawaiians were celebrating the annual makahiki (festival) of the god Lono. Captain Cook was immediately mistaken for that god, and given a very friendly welcome! According to Cook there must have been a thousand canoes around his ships, with people swimming in the water like schools of fish. The British stayed for several weeks to get provisions for their crews and to study the Hawaiians. In early February they left, but soon had to return because a storm damaged one of their vessels and repairs were needed. This was a fateful move. Tensions had built up, and the returning British were not as warmly welcomed by the natives. A minor incident started a battle at the shore between the Hawaiians and the British in which Captain Cook was stabbed to death. People on both sides were saddened by this. The Hawaiians treated Cook's body with the respect given that of a great ali'i. Some of this bones were returned to his ships. The rest were stored in sacred heiau elsewhere on the island. Thus the first recorded contact between Hawai'i and the outside world ended in tragedy.

Other explorers soon followed Captain Cook. In the meantime, major events were occurring within Hawai'i itself. A brilliant warrior, Kamehameha I, conquered most of the main islands, and created the kingdom of Hawai'i. By 1810 all the islands were under his control.

In 1820, when the first Christian missionaries arrived, the immigration of settlers from America and Europe had already begun. Life for the Hawaiians would never be the same. The ancient kapu system had been abolished by King Kamehameha II even before the arrival of the first missionaries. The 'ohana were broken apart as the Western system of land ownership was introduced, and young people moved to the growing towns. Diseases that foreigners could resist killed thousands of Hawaiians who hadn't developed natural resistance to them. By 1884 there were more non-Hawaiians than Hawaiians living in the Islands! The old ways of life were forever gone, and the Hawaiian population was rapidly decreasing. In 1893 a revolution overthrew the Kingdom of Hawai'i, and in 1898, the Islands officially became a Territory of the United States. In 1959, Hawai'i became America's 50th state, 181 years after its discovery by Captain Cook.

In spite of the changes, many aspects of the old ways of life have survived to enhance modern society. Among other things, the early Hawaiians enjoyed the sport of surfing, hula dancing, the art of making flower lei, the lū'au (which they called 'aha'aina), and the spirit of aloha—or warm generosity and friendliness to be shared with others. We owe much to the early Hawaiians. By visiting places like Pu'uhonua o Hōnaunau, you may better understand and appreciate how these people lived.

Captain James Cook,
Royal British Navy

Decline of the Heiau...

A.D. 1750

SAME SCENE, 200 YEARS LATER

..and their importance to us today

The first non-Hawaiians to visit Pu'uhonua o Hōnaunau were men of Captain Cook's expedition in 1779. The next "outsider" to visit was a botanist, Archibald Menzies, who traveled with the British expedition of Captain George Vancouver in 1793. These men saw the pu'uhonua when it was a place of refuge and a mausoleum for the Keawe chiefs.

During the 30 years following Vancouver's expedition, great changes took place in Hawaiian society. Many people of Hawai'i embraced Christianity and threw away their traditional ways of life, especially the rigid system of kapu laws upon which the pu'uhonua system was based. In 1819, Liholiho, the son and heir of Kamehameha I, formally abolished the ancient religion of Hawai'i, including its kapu laws. He ordered that the heiau be destroyed. Hundreds of temple images, structures, and other artifacts were torn apart or burned. Much that could have been of value today in teaching us about ancient Hawai'i was lost.

Despite this destruction, Hale o Keawe still stood when the Reverend William Ellis visited Hōnaunau in 1823.

Two years later a caretaker permitted officers from the British ship H.M.S. Blonde to enter Hale o Keawe and take anything they wished, except for the bones of ali'i. Neglected and unmaintained, the house fell apart in later years.

When the U. S. National Park Service started its project to restore Pu'uhonua o Hōnaunau in 1961, the drawings and observations made by these early visitors, and the artifacts they saved by collecting, were almost the only clues available as to the original appearance of the pu'uhonua. Fortunately there was enough information to allow an accurate reconstruction of such important features as the Great Wall and Hale o Keawe.

Why should we be concerned with restoring and preserving Pu'uhonua o Hōnaunau, or for that matter anything that reminds us of our past history? A major reason is that such places provide us with an accurate glimpse of the way we once lived. They help us know and understand the truth about our past. This can be helpful in preventing misconceptions and misunderstandings among people today. Furthermore, they can give us a comfortable feeling of knowing where we fit in the long story of human history. We can indentify directly with our ancestors by visiting the places of their handiwork.

Pu'uhonua o Hōnaunau National Historical Park preserves a physical fragment of an ancient way of life that is forever gone, but which still influences us in many ways today.

ANSWERS TO QUESTIONS AND PUZZLES:

Page 18) Petroglyph: A man

Page 22) Here are some examples of some English words which changed their meaning greatly through time:

STARS was once used exclusively to refer to points of light in the night sky, and to a person's fortune. Now it is used to signify celebrities as well.

BRAKES once was widely used to refer to thickets of vegetation. Now it is more widely used to signify a component of automobiles.

BY AND BY This expression once meant "immediately"; now it means "after a while," just the opposite meaning!

GULLS used to signify unfeathered birds, such as chicks, in general, rather than the familiar species of shorebird itself.

TO BE IN DEBT used to mean "to be in danger," rather than simply owing something to someone.

PLUS NUMEROUS COLLOQUIAL WORDS AND EXPRESSIONS!

Page 22) Word Scramble:

WORD SCRAMBLE

```
O L U A L O A N K K A L K A U
M N O O K O N U P E N A K O A
N T O N O K K U U A M L N O O
H U W N O U A O W A W E N O P
K E P P I W U I A U I A P A A
A M L C I W U I P P L L A P E
M A P E O O N M A U O E H A I
E N U N I A O O W N P A O P O
H A A W O P U U T A P P E A U
A N N A K N A W W I U I H N O
M O N U L M H L N P A W O E W
E O W K A P A L A A O P E L E
H K I E P P L P P L O K E A W
A L O I A A A L A H A O P N M
M A U N A L O A O K E A L A N
L C P P A U A K I L O A M I M
L O N A I M U H A W A I I N N
O O N U I K A U A I O W N K O
K K O O U L E M E L E N N I M
I I W I I K A P O N O H A W U
```

Page 46) Connect the dots: "ALOHA!"

Page 48) Archaeology hunt: Look for parts of
  a) a stone musical instrument with two holes
  b) a calabash
  c) a ki'i (wooden image)
  d) a tooth necklace
  e) a kōnane board
  f) a spear tip
  g) a flute
  h) a fishhook

Page 51) Connect the dots: a lei (flower garland)

Page 59) Pōhaku Ki'i
  a) this is a figure with a headdress, possibly an ali'i
  b) this may be a row of marching warriors
  c) this looks like a pair of boxers
  d) typical male figure with triangular body
  e) sea turtle
  f) the head of this figure is arched by a symbol representing a rainbow. Like figure (a) this could be an ali'i. Rainbows were associated with the mana of ali'i.

Page 65) Hawaiian crossword;
  Across: 1) Hawai'i, 3) Aloha, 5) Ali'i, 7) Kōnane, 9) Poi, 13) Hala, 15) Pu'u, 17) Kahuna, 19) 'Opihi, 20) Ahupua'a, 23) Hula

  Down: 2) Mana, 4) Aloha, 6) 'Aina, 7) Kī, 10) 'Ohana, 12) 'Ohia, 14) Niu, 16) Heiau, 17) Kū, 18) Hōnaunau, 20) Ipu, 22) Kapu, 24) Ulua, 25) Makahiki

Page 67) The large rocks strewn across the flats near the shore were thrown up by storm waves, and possibly tsunami which ripped the rocks from the shoreline and seafloor nearby.

Page 67) a) The Hawaiians may have constructed a small doorway to help keep the sacred mana and spirits associated with the bones of the ali'i safely inside Hale o Keawe.

  b) They are mean-looking to command respect by instilling fear in the peole who visited the heiau.

  c) The ridge-like markings were made when the molten lava which enveloped the log oozed into grooves in the bark, cooled and solidified.

  d) It takes less energy to put the heaviest, largest rocks on the bottom. Also, this configuration may be more stable; if the large rocks were on top, there could be more chance the structure would collapse as small rocks at the base are weathered out and removed.

  e) The roof was thatched this way to allow rainwater to flow off the outside of the building, and not seep inside.

THANKS TO

The staffs of Pu'uhonua o Hōnaunau National Historical Park and the Hawai'i Natural History Association, and to the works of Peter Buck, J. Halley Cox, Samuel Kamakau, Donald D. Kilolani Mitchell, Mary K. Pukui, and Edward Stasek, without whose contributions this booklet could not have been produced.

A REVIEW

Here are some questions about Pu'uhonua o Honaunau. If you've read this book, you may be able to answer them. Test yourself to see how well you do! The answers are listed at the bottom of the page, upside down.

1) "Pu'uhonua" is a Hawaiian word meaning _____

2) Why did the Hawaiians store the bones of royalty at Hale o Keawe?

3) What may have been the purpose of The Great Wall?

4) "To break kapu" meant...

5) Who was the British sea captain who "discovered" Hawai'i in 1778?

6) The land in ancient Hawai'i was divided into "ahupua'a." These were typically:
   a) square areas of land.
   b) narrow strips of land confined to the coast.
   c) wedge-shaped areas of land, extending from the sea, through the forest belt, to the high mountains.
   d) circular plots of land with pu'uhonua at the center of each.

7) Why was the system of dividing land into ahupua'a fair for the early Hawaiians?

8) Hawaiians took the bark of the wauke (paper mulberry) to make a type of cloth called _____.

9) Explain the duties of a konohiki

10) What were the two types of transportation in ancient Hawai'i?

11) Who were the kāhuna?

1) "Pu'uhonua" means "place of refuge." (2) An important reason is that the Hawaiians believed the mana, or spiritual power, of the bones gave additional protection to the pu'uhonua. (3) The Great Wall marks the boundary at Pu'uhonua o Honaunau. It may also have been built to further discourage pursuers from entering the place of refuge. (4) "To break kapu" meant to break the sacred way of doing things in ancient Hawai'i, (5) Captain James Cook, (6)(c), (7)It allowed most Hawaiians approximately equal access to natural resources, (8) Kapa (or tapa), (9) The konohiki was the administrator and tax collector of the ahupua'a. He supervised major community projects, such as building irrigation works, and bringing fishing. During war, he also conscripted soldiers for the ali'i. He saw after the well-being of the ahupua'a, (10) Canoes, and movement on foot, (11) Kāhuna were persons with special training and skills. The priests were one category of kāhuna.

72

The End